THE ESSENTIAL GUIDE
TO HIGH QUALITY CURRICULUM
AND INSTRUCTION:

HANDBOOK FOR
TEXAS TEACHERS AND LEADERS

BY

JOHN A. CRAIN

The Essential Guide to High Quality Curriculum and Instruction: Handbook for Texas Teachers and Leaders

First Printing: August, 2018

Copyright © ED311

ED311
The Leader in Education Resources.

512 W Martin Luther King Jr Blvd, #300 Austin, TX 78701
Phone 512-478-2113
Fax 512-495-9955
www.ed311.com I info@ed311.com

ISBN 978-1-947753-04-4

ACKNOWLEDGEMENTS

Everything I know I learned from great teachers, mentors, and writers.

Jim Boyd was the Dean of Education at Tarleton State University and later president of Weatherford College. Thank you, Jim, for translating learning theory into practice and teaching an entire generation of educators to be instructional leaders. You were my friend and mentor and were a critical turning point in my learning and my life.

Madeline Hunter was for many years a professor of education and psychology at the University of California-Los Angeles. Her academic background was in psychology. Her life's work was taking what she found in psychological research and translating it to classroom practice. On a snowy night at Dallas-Ft. Worth International Airport, as we drank wine and ate nachos, she said to me, "I am not an original thinker. I just try to take the theory and translate it into practice." Her approach is the model which I have feebly attempted to emulate.

Lorin Anderson and David Krathwohl published *A Taxonomy for Learning, Teaching, and Assessing: A Revision of Bloom's Taxonomy of Educational Objectives* (2001). Their work has had significant impact on my thinking about curriculum. I have quoted liberally from their work, and I am grateful for their pioneering work. At times, I may have slightly departed from some of their conclusions.

Richard James is curriculum specialist at Region 10 Education Service Center in Richardson; **Regina Reed** is the former director of English Language Arts in Allen ISD. They are my go-to experts on all things dealing with curriculum and instruction when I need my own thinking tested and challenged. As critical, thoughtful editors, they are without peer.

No one can be an expert in every academic discipline. Thankfully, I have friends who are. Many of the academic content examples in this book were suggested by **Jane Silvey, Donna**

Edwards Wise, Amy Smith, and Jean Gill. Debbie Estes was a great resource and critical reader of the sections on brain research and retention of learning. **Kathy Kee** is a dear friend, mentor, and guru on coaching. As always, she provided much-needed encouragement for my efforts and feedback on the content. **Regina Conroy** has led schools and coached teachers and campus administrators for many years. I am grateful for her input into the chapter on learning environment and classroom norms.

Ron Simpson is a master at creating visual representations of complex learning. I am greatly appreciative of his graphics for deductive and inductive learning.

Patrick and Deb Cates are a two-person Seal Team among editors. Patrick is a former high school English and principal at Highland Park High School. Deb is a former middle school English teacher. I am grateful for their zeal and expertise in editing the final manuscript. Any remaining errors are mine.

I have been blessed to have many great teachers and a few awful ones. I have learned from all of you. Among the great ones: **Tom Vickery**, high school English teacher, who was the first teacher who challenged me to think; **Carroll Hickey**, friend and college debate coach who taught me formal logic and pushed me farther than I thought I could go; **William Russel**, university professor and Anglican priest who instilled in me a love of learning for the sake of learning; and the many professors of education at Midwestern State University who tolerated my youthful arrogance.

Finally, my gratitude to the **Brothers of Holy Cross** and the **Sisters of St. Mary of Namur**. In my beginning years as a teacher, you were models of excellence in teaching and love of students. In particular, my thanks to **Brother Richard Daly, CSC** who took a chance and gave me my first opportunity to teach. He is both a friend and mentor.

INTRODUCTION

As you will see, this book was not written as a traditional academic textbook. My goal was to write a handbook that is easy and friendly to read—a kind of everyday handbook for teachers and leaders. While I referenced research sources, I have attempted not to clutter the narrative with myriad footnotes/endnotes. For those of you who want to read more academic theory, there is a works cited list at the end of each chapter.

Sometimes there is a tension, particularly in higher education, between theory and practice. Here's my position: theory without application to actual classroom practice is meaningless for what you do every day. At the same time, practice that is not based on good theory and research is suspect and should be viewed with suspicion. I have great respect for academic research and theory. As a result, I have relied on some of the best research theory and expertise available. My goal was then to translate and synthesize that theory into practice—what you do every day with students.

I intentionally chose my style of writing to talk <u>to</u> you—not to write <u>at</u> you. Hence, this handbook is written in the first person. If the style bothers you, I apologize.

You will find lots of informal language. Sometimes the technical vocabulary of our pedagogy seems to serve as a gatekeeper that <u>prevents</u> us from understanding. Some may conclude that I have oversimplified some very complex issues. To that, I plead semi-guilty! If you find the informal (occasionally over-the-top!) style and language irritating, I ask your indulgence and forgiveness.

If you are a formal leader (principal, assistant principal, instructional coach), I hope that you will find information and tools to support you as you coach and lead. When I frequently use the pronoun you, take off your administrator hat for a moment and put your teacher hat back on—I think you will find that the hat still fits! If you are a beginning teacher, I hope that this book will help you organize your prior learning and, perhaps, add some things to your tool kit. If your undergraduate preparation focused on the theories of teaching/learning, I hope that you see the practices that stem from it. If your teacher preparation was primarily based on practice ("do this; don't do that"), I am hopeful that you will discover the theory on which those practices are based. If you are an experienced teacher, I hope that you will find in this book information that validates your practice and that helps you articulate why you are a good teacher. If you can articulate what makes you effective, you will be a more intentional, thoughtful, and reflective practitioner. If you want to be an even better teacher, perhaps this book can serve as a diagnostic tool for your practice and offer new alternatives for how you understand curriculum and instruction.

My primary goal is to support your noble quest to design rich, rigorous, meaningful, and joyous learning for the students you love and serve.

TABLE OF CONTENTS

Chapter 6: Students Do Something With the Stuff

Chapter 7: Students Demonstrate That They Have Learned

Chapter 8: Learning Environment and Classroom Management ... 101

CHAPTER 1

CURRICULUM OVERVIEW

What is Curriculum?

Many of us who have been in education for more than a few years have been asked this question many times. However, just the notion of having to read about curriculum may have you groaning. Halfway through the chapter your groans may shift to moaning. That's understandable. Even though we may not all aspire to be curriculum geeks, this first chapter will provide a foundation to further your thinking about curriculum and the role it plays in education. As a teacher, you are all about students. Your passion is designing wonderful lessons that engage their interests and that result in joyous learning that stimulates their thinking. Good for you! Fifty years in education has taught me that when we ignore or, worse, do not understand curriculum, learning may be joyous and interesting, but it can frequently result in unfocused learning and/or learning that lacks real depth and complexity. I recall training sessions with curriculum guru Fenwick English in which he told us, "Curriculum doesn't matter unless it makes no difference what students are learning."

So, while I do not recommend it, here's an option. At least read the section in this chapter on Performance Standards and Content Standards. Then skip the chapters on curriculum and go straight to Chapter 4 on lesson design. Then come back to the parts of this chapter that you need to dig a little deeper in and understand better. Having given you the permission that you do not need, let's get started.

Every state has some version of curriculum or curriculum standards. In Texas, these standards are the Texas Essential Knowledge and Skills (TEKS), and local school districts are required to teach them (Texas Education Code - EDUC § 39.0236). The curriculum is defined and required by both the state and your school district by way of the TEKS: a series of learning objective statements that contain a performance standard and content standard. The instructional component should belong to you. The instruction consists of the activities, strategies, materials, and resources that you will use as the delivery vehicle for the curriculum. Herein lies the difference between curriculum and instruction.

In hand-in-hand partnership with the curriculum is instruction. Figure 1 is intended to provide you with a mental picture to help differentiate between curriculum and instruction.

Figure 1

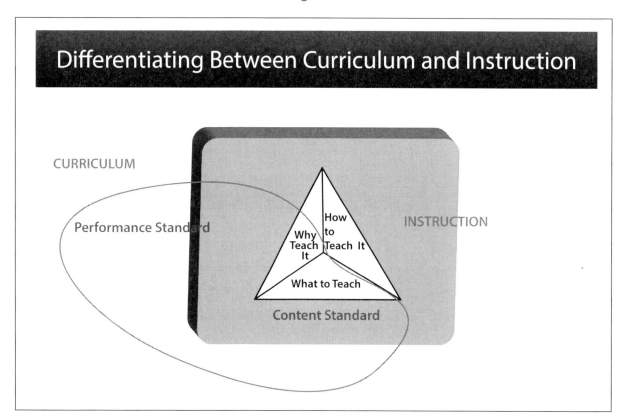

When I ask most educators, "What is curriculum?" the most common answer I get is "curriculum is what we teach." The second most common answer is "curriculum is what we teach and the strategies and resources we use." These answers blur the clarity of what curriculum really is. Allow me to offer the following definition: Curriculum is a set of learner standards that contain two elements--a performance standard and a content standard. Consider the following example:

The student is expected to: analyze the major issues and events of the Vietnam War such as the Tet Offensive, the escalation of forces, Vietnamization, and the fall of Saigon (U.S. History, high school, Texas Essential Knowledge and Skills).

Essentially, the curriculum statement says, "The student is expected to 'verb some stuff'." In curriculum terminology, the verb (and its modifiers)" is called a Performance Standard. The "stuff" is called a Content Standard.

A CURRICULUM STANDARD HAS TWO COMPONENTS:

1. A PERFORMANCE STANDARD (THE VERB AND ITS MODIFIERS) AND

2. A CONTENT STANDARD (THE ACADEMIC CONTENT)

Based on my definition of curriculum, the history example from above should be broken down as follows:

Performance Standard: *(verb)* Analyze

Content Standard: *(some stuff)* the major issues and events of the Vietnam War such as the Tet Offensive, the escalation of forces, Vietnamization, and the fall of Saigon

That's what <u>curriculum</u> is: a performance standard and a content standard—something students should know and be able to do. In public and public charter schools, the curriculum is determined by the state and school district and is non-negotiable—you are required to follow it. In most of the national literature on curriculum, you will find that a "guaranteed" curriculum is one of the hallmarks of successful schools. It guarantees that all students will have the opportunity to learn a common set of standards. The <u>instruction</u> is a completely separate issue. In some school districts, the organization attempts to create so-called "teacher-proof curriculum and instruction." I believe that this practice is rooted, in part, on a lack of confidence in the quality of the instruction: "Just follow the curriculum, use the lessons and resources, and all will be well." My experience is that this is rarely true, yet some districts persist in attempting to control and standardize all the learning variables: curriculum, instruction, resources, and assessment.

If the instruction in your district is prescribed and required, it is usually on the district's "curriculum" web site or curriculum portal. Both the curriculum and instruction (and sometimes the resources and assessments) are all included under the umbrella of "curriculum." This information can create some confusion about which elements you are required to use. You must deliver the curriculum. That is always required. The other elements (instruction, resources, assessment, etc.) may or may not be required locally. Check with your district/campus administration to find out what is required.

Thankfully, in most school districts, the instruction belongs to the teacher. The message to teachers on instruction is "teach the curriculum in whatever ways fit your teaching style and, especially, your students' learning styles." That means that three different teachers could be teaching the same curriculum is three entirely different ways. There is one *caveat*: the students must learn the curriculum. After all that we know about what works in schools, we are, hopefully, at the end of the discussion which argued, "Well, I taught the curriculum, but the students just didn't learn it. They didn't study. They didn't do their homework. They didn't pay attention in class, etc." No, no, no! If most of the students did not learn the curriculum, most often the fault lies with the instruction which is designed by the teacher. Granted, there are many variables that influence student success. Many are beyond the control of the classroom teacher; however, what teachers do have control over must be managed as efficiently and effectively as possible. *Aligning curriculum and instruction is one of the most important* variables you control. This is a difficult proposition for many teachers to accept. Most teachers show up every day doing 100% of what they know how to do and are comfortable doing. If you are not doing what you should be doing, it may be that you don't know what you should be doing, or you know what you should be doing but don't know how to do it. This is certainly true of student-centered instruction. The Texas Teacher Evaluation and Support System (T-TESS) has a scoring bias that ranges from teacher-centered instruction on the low end of the scoring rubric and student-centered instruction on the high end of the scoring rubric. So, most of you have the idea that student-centered instruction is best practice; the question is whether or not you have the knowledge and skills to plan and implement student-centered instruction.

The reality is that to be able to effectively design and deliver instruction for your students, you have to have the following:

- A deep and thorough knowledge of the academic content that you teach

- An intimate, reflective understanding of your teaching style

- A deep, thorough, and respectful knowledge of your students and how they learn/don't learn

- A knowledge of strategies and best practices in teaching, especially those practices that turn the work, thinking, and learning over to the students

1. Curriculum Tells You What Students Must Know and What They Are Expected to Do With What They Know

1. Following the Curriculum is Required by Law

1. A Guaranteed Curriculum Assures Curricular Equity

1. A Guaranteed, Aligned Curriculum Decreases Learning Gaps and Unproductive Redundancies

Why is The Curriculum Important?

Curriculum Tells You What Students Must Know and What They Are Expected to Do With What They Know

Note that every curriculum standard begins with the phrase "The student is expected to…." As a teacher, the standard describes what your students are expected to <u>know</u> and what they are <u>expected to do</u> with the content knowledge.

Thinking about the previous history curriculum example, your specific role as a teacher is to design instruction for this curriculum standard to ensure that your students (1) learn the content knowledge about the Vietnam War and (2) analyze that content knowledge. Your role is **not** to do the analysis of the content knowledge and then ask the students to regurgitate your analysis on some kind of assignment or assessment. Your role is to design activities in which **all of the students** are doing the analyzing, usually in pairs or groups.

Following the Curriculum is Required by Law

As I noted at the beginning of the chapter, both state law and your district's policy require you to teach the curriculum: Texas Essential Knowledge and Skills (TEKS) (Texas Education Code - EDUC § 39.0236). Failure to follow the curriculum is a violation of state law and district policy which is grounds for contract nonrenewal. As an ethical and professional person, choose the lane for ethical conduct.

A Guaranteed Curriculum Assures Curricular Equity

Not every school district has equitable resources. Some have more money to spend and are able to purchase mounds of materials, hire highly trained teachers, and provide a variety of learning experiences for students. Others have to struggle to provide even the most basic resources. Some districts are populated by predominately middle- or upper-middle class students, while others are populated predominately by economically disadvantaged students, many of whom are the product of generational (as opposed to situational) poverty. Regardless of these factors, the state guarantees, through the TEKS, that every student in the state will have the opportunity to learn a rigorous curriculum. Even within a single school, there may significant differences among teachers. Some are effective, veteran teachers. Others may be novices who are overwhelmed with the demands of interpreting the curriculum and designing the instruction while trying to manage classroom behavior. It is therefore almost impossible to guarantee <u>instructional</u> equity. With a guaranteed, legally-required curriculum, your school can at least guarantee <u>curriculum standard</u> equity—every student has the opportunity to learn the approved and adopted curriculum.

A Guaranteed, Aligned Curriculum Deceases Learning Gaps and Unproductive Redundancies

Why can't you just teach whatever you want to teach? If you do that, you open up the probability that you will unintentionally create gaps and unproductive redundancies in your students' knowledge and skills. For example, the science curriculum in grades K-8 is "general science": some earth science, some life science, and some physical science (chemistry and physics). Without a defined, aligned curriculum, students may be taught within your comfort zone: lots of life science, some earth science, but very little physical science. This would create a huge gap in your students' foundational concepts in chemistry and physics. Potentially, students may arrive at high school chemistry and physics with little or no academic foundation in these subjects, causing them to struggle and underperform at this level.

Teaching whatever you want to teach may also create unproductive redundancies. This consequence occurs when teachers have "love units." You just love having students write haikus. Sadly, writing haikus is <u>not</u> part of your curriculum—it's the curriculum for the next grade level! But still you decide to spend significant time having students write haikus. How many years in a row do students need to see a butterfly evolve through their life cycle or watch a lima bean sprout in a moist paper towel? Generally, once is probably enough. After spending time on these "love units," you then complain (although perhaps with some justification) that you just don't have enough time to teach the required curriculum!

Summary

- Curriculum is the beginning point for your planning. Curriculum standards have two components:

  - A performance standard (the verb and its modifiers)—what students are expected to do with the content standard (the stuff)

  - A content standard (the academic content—the stuff)

- The curriculum standards are determined by the state and the school district—they are non-negotiable.

- The instruction is the delivery system for the curriculum. The instruction belongs to you. Teach the curriculum however you want as long as the students can successfully learn it that way.

- Why The Curriculum is Important

  ◦ Curriculum tells you what students must know and what they are expected to do with what they know.

  ◦ A non-negotiable, guaranteed curriculum assures curricular equity—all students have the opportunity to learn a rigorous curriculum.

  ◦ A guaranteed, aligned curriculum decreases learning gaps and unproductive redundancies as students progress through the curriculum.

Most teacher evaluation systems express some expectation about your use of the curriculum. Obviously, you want to know and follow your district's expectations. As you analyze the curriculum, ask yourself these questions:

1. Am I already thinking about activities that are fully aligned with the state goals and curriculum content standards?

2. Beyond what I already know, what additionally do I need to learn about the content standard?

3. How can I integrate academic content from other curriculum areas so that students recognize the connectivity across disciplines?

4. How can I design a lesson so that all students actively engaged in activities that require a variety of deep, complex thinking?

5. How can I design assessments for learning that are aligned with the curriculum and instruction?

Descriptors from Texas Teacher Evaluation and Support System (T-TESS) Related to Curriculum Planning

From the T-TESS Scoring Guide

<u>Standards and Alignment</u>

Dimension 1.1: The teacher designs clear, well-organized, sequential lessons that reflect best practice, align with standards and are appropriate for diverse learners.

- All goals aligned to state content standards.

- All objectives aligned to the lesson's goal.

<u>Content Knowledge and Expertise</u>

Dimension 2.2: The teacher uses content and pedagogical expertise to design and execute lessons aligned with state standards, related content and student needs.

- Conveys accurate content knowledge in multiple contexts.

- Integrates learning objectives with other disciplines.

- Provides opportunities for students to use different types of thinking (e.g., analytical, practical).

- Accurately reflects how the lesson fits within the structure of the discipline and the state standards.

Disclaimer: The descriptors from T-TESS are exactly as they appear in the *T-TESS Scoring Guide.* Sadly, the writers of T-TESS chose to abandon the sacred Oxford Comma for items in series. For those of you who care, the Oxford Comma is the comma before the "and" for items in a series.

Works Referenced

Texas Education Agency (2016). *Texas teacher evaluation and support system: T-TESS appraiser handbook.* Austin, TX.

Texas Education Code - EDUC § 39.0236

CHAPTER 2

CONTENT STANDARDS AND THE THREE DOMAINS OF CURRICULUM

This chapter deals with the content standard (the stuff) in the curriculum. As you will see, the content is dependent on which of the three domains of curriculum you are teaching.

THREE DOMAINS OF CURRICULUM

1. DOMAIN 1: COGNITIVE LEARNING

2. DOMAIN 2: AFFECTIVE LEARNING

3. DOMAIN 3: PSYCHOMOTOR LEARNING

Traditionally, curriculum has been divided into three domains or classifications: cognitive, affective, and psychomotor. While the domains frequently overlap, I will present them here as though they are separate and unrelated—clearly an oversimplification of some very complex issues.

These three domains are characterized by significant differences in the content standard (the stuff).

Curriculum Domain 1: Cognitive Learning

Cognitive learning can informally be described as acquiring and processing knowledge. Students get the stuff and "process" the stuff. The "processes" may be at any of the six levels Blooms Taxonomy of Cognitive Learning. Note that when most of us use the phrase "Bloom's Taxonomy," we are usually referring to his taxonomy of <u>cognitive</u> learning. Bloom also has a taxonomy of affective learning—more about that in a bit. In the core curriculum (mathematics, science, social studies, reading/ELA), virtually the entire curriculum is in the cognitive domain. That is not the case in other areas such as Career and Technical Education (CTE), health/physical education, and the visual and performing arts.

The content standard (stuff) in cognitive learning may be:

- Factual Knowledge
- Conceptual Knowledge
- Procedural Knowledge

This terminology comes from the work of Anderson, *et. al.* The interpretations and commentary are mine.

Here are some examples of the stuff (content standard) in cognitive learning from the core curriculum. Note that I have struck through the performance standard; what remains is the content standard.

<u>Cognitive Learning: Factual Knowledge</u>

Figure 1

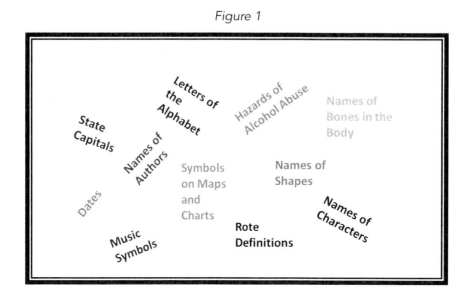

Definition of Factual Knowledge (Anderson, et al)	Example	Commentary
Factual knowledge may be distinguished from conceptual knowledge by virtue of its very specificity; that is, factual knowledge can be isolated as elements or bits of information that are believed to have some value in and of themselves.	~~identify~~ the accomplishments of individuals and groups such as Jane Addams, Susan B. Anthony, Dwight Eisenhower, Martin Luther King Jr., Rosa Parks, Cesar Chavez, Franklin D. Roosevelt, Ronald Reagan, Colin Powell, the Tuskegee Airmen, and the 442nd Regimental Combat Team who have made contributions to society in the areas of civil rights, women's rights, military actions, and politics. (5th Grade History – Texas Essential Knowledge and Skills)	Except for social studies, there are virtually <u>no</u> content standards (stuff) that are factual knowledge in the core curriculum (mathematics, science, ELA/Reading). Most of the content standards (stuff) in the core curriculum are either conceptual or procedural. Figure 1 contains some examples of factual knowledge.

Cognitive Learning: Conceptual Knowledge

Figure 2

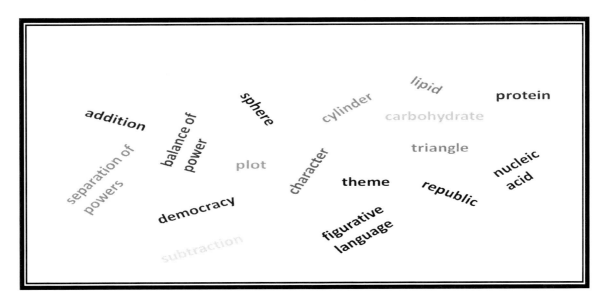

Definition of Conceptual Knowledge (Anderson, et al)	Examples All examples are from the Texas Essential Knowledge and Skills (TEKS) Note: To emphasize the content standard, I am striking through the performance standard/verb.	Commentary
"Conceptual knowledge includes knowledge of categories and classifications and relationships between and among them…. Conceptual knowledge includes schemas (*and*) mental models…. …. (*It*) might be one aspect of what is termed "disciplinary knowledge," or the way experts in the discipline think…."	~~model~~ the relationship between the volume of a cylinder and a cone having both congruent bases and heights and connect that relationship to the formulas (8th Grade Mathematics) ~~use~~ concrete models to count fractional parts beyond one whole using words and ~~recognize~~ how many parts it takes to equal one whole (2nd Grade Mathematics) ~~analyze and evaluate~~ the relationship of natural selection to adaptation and to the development of diversity in and among species (High School Biology) ~~describe~~ the interaction of characters including their relationships and the changes they undergo (3rd Grade English Language Arts and Reading) ~~describe and explain~~ the effects of physical environmental processes such as erosion, ocean currents, and earthquakes on Earth's surface (6th Grade Social Studies)	These concepts are sometimes thought of as the "big ideas" or the central themes and concepts of a discipline. In physical science, students will be dealing with the concepts of "force and motion" from elementary school through graduate school in physics. The same is true of the study of literature. Students will be dealing with the concept of "author's point of view" in elementary school and will still be dealing with that concept in graduate school. The complexity and sophistication with which they are asked to apply these concepts will increase; however, the concepts remain the same throughout the students' learning journey. These listed in Figure 2 are a few examples of curriculum in which the content standard is conceptual.

Cognitive Learning: Procedural Knowledge

Figure 3

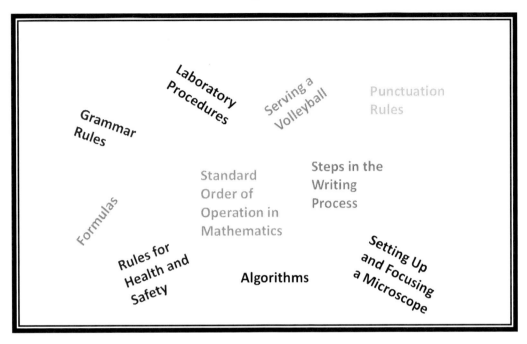

Definition of Conceptual Knowledge (Anderson, et al)	Examples All examples are from the Texas Essential Knowledge and Skills (TEKS) Note: To emphasize the content standard in all examples, I am striking through the performance standard.	Commentary
"How to do something; methods of inquiry, and criteria for using skills, algorithms, techniques, methods."	Mathematics ~~use~~ a problem-solving model that incorporates analyzing given information, formulating a plan or strategy, determining a solution, justifying the solution, and evaluating the problem-solving process and the reasonableness of the solution (4th Grade Mathematics) ~~calculate~~ unit rates from rates in mathematical and real-world problems (7th Grade Mathematics) Science ~~express and manipulate~~ chemical quantities using scientific conventions and mathematical procedures, including dimensional analysis, scientific notation, and significant figures (High School Chemistry).	In mathematics the content standards (stuff) may be conceptual, procedural, or both. In all mathematics curriculum standards, there are never standards that are only procedural; if there is a procedure, there is always a concept behind that procedure. In grades K-2, virtually all the mathematics content standards (stuff) are completely conceptual; there are none that requires computation. In grades 3-12, the content standard tends to be to be both conceptual and sometimes procedural.

	ELA/R ~~recognize and use~~ punctuation marks including commas in compound sentences and quotation marks (4th Grade ELA/R) ~~recognize and use~~ punctuation marks including commas in compound sentences and quotation marks (4th Grade ELA/R) ~~use~~ elements of the writing process (planning, drafting, revising, editing, and publishing) to compose text (7th Grade ELA/R) ~~use~~ elements of the writing process (planning, drafting, revising, editing, and publishing) to compose text (7th Grade ELA/R) Social Studies ~~locate~~ places using the four cardinal directions (1st Grade Social Studies). ~~use~~ a problem-solving process to identify a problem, gather information, list and consider options, consider advantages and disadvantages, choose and implement a solution, and evaluate the effectiveness of the solution (High School Government).	Much of the procedural knowledge in both mathematics and science is in the so-called "process standards." These sets of skills call upon students to follow steps and rules in problem-solving and decision-making. Remember, I am talking about the <u>content</u> standard that represents following procedures (steps and rules). In English language arts/reading, the procedural knowledge (following steps and/or rules) is represented in two ways. First, there are curriculum standards in which the content standard is clearly procedural. For the most part this procedural knowledge is contained in the writing TEKS, e.g. the writing process and language mechanics (grammar, capitalization, spelling, and punctuation). Figure 3 provides some examples of procedural learning.

Finally, there is a set of thinking process skills embedded in what has been known as Figure 19. In the 2019-2020 ELA/R TEKS, these skills are included within the curriculum, not as a separate set—yay!! From my perspective, reading comprehension is always about thinking.

- **Reading Comprehension Skills**

    ○ monitor comprehension and make adjustments such as re-reading, using background knowledge, asking questions, and annotating when understanding breaks down (5th Grade ELA/R).

    ○ make inferences and use evidence to support understanding (High School English II).

- **Response Skills**

    ◦ interact with sources in meaningful ways such as notetaking, annotating, freewriting, or illustrating (8th Grade ELA/R)

    ◦ defend or challenge the authors' claims using relevant text evidence (High School English II)

Curriculum Domain 2: Affective Learning

Affective Learning is the <u>overt</u> teaching of values. That is different from the general sense of things such as modeling courtesy and respect. Affective curriculum is generally written and is very intentional. The content standards may be:

- Attitudes

- Values

- Beliefs

- Judgments

In the four core areas (mathematics, science, social studies and ELA/Reading), 90%+ of the content standards are in the cognitive domain of knowledge. While the subject areas outside the core curriculum contain content standards in the cognitive domain, they are replete with content standards that overtly and intentionally teach students to hold and exhibit defined attitudes, values, beliefs, and judgments. Here are some examples of curriculum statements in the affective domain. To emphasize that I am addressing the content standard, I am continuing to strike through the performance standard.

<u>Career and Technical Education (CTE)</u>

- ~~compare and contrast~~ animal rights and animal welfare (Small Animal Management).

    The content standard clearly asks students to make value judgments about animal rights and welfare.

- ~~explain~~ the characteristics of personal values and principles (Culinary Arts).

    Again, the content standard involves defining and explaining "personal values and principles."

<u>Health Education</u>

Particularly in the area of health and wellness, the success of the teaching/learning involves making choices about personal lifestyle. For example.

- ~~identify and describe~~ strategies for avoiding drugs, violence, gangs, weapons, and other harmful situations (6th Grade Health).

The content standard calls on students to develop strategies for avoiding drugs, violence, weapons, and other harmful situations. The student will likely develop many options from which to choose, depending on their own value system and life experiences.

<u>Visual and Performing Arts</u>

- ~~Explore and communicate~~ ideas drawn from life experiences about self, peers, family, school, or community and from the imagination as sources for original works of art (4th Grade Art)

Wow! The content standard will differ significantly from student to student: their life experiences and imagination expressed in a work if art! Again, the student's own value system, experience, and imagination determine what will be communicated and how it will be communicated.

Curriculum Domain 3: Psychomotor Learning

Psychomotor Learning involves physical skills or tasks. Wilson, The Peak Performance Center, and others have offered great insight into the various kinds of psychomotor learning. The content standard (the stuff) might be:

- movement

- coordination

- manipulation

- dexterity

- grace

- strength

Playing a musical instrument, dance, handwriting, fine motor skills, and a whole variety of sports activities all involve psychomotor learning. Remember that the domains are not always clearly separated. For example, playing a musical instrument involves psychomotor skills (e.g., feet, fingers, diaphragm/breath control, etc.). Generally, it also requires that the student can read the music (cognitive learning), and performing with expression (affective learning). Some content standards that are primarily in the psychomotor domain include:

- ~~demonstrate~~ proper form and smooth transitions during combinations of fundamental locomotor and body control skills such as running and jumping safely in dynamic situations (3rd Grade Physical Education)

- ~~create~~ rhythmic phrases ~~using known rhythms and melodic phrases using known pitches at an appropriate level of difficulty~~ (Middle School Music).

Note: "Rhythmic phrases" is the content standard. Sometimes the performance standard includes the verb <u>and</u> other words that modify the verb. Those modifiers are, therefore, part of the performance standard.

- ~~invent~~ images that combine a variety of lines, shapes, colors, textures, and forms (1st Grade Art).

As before, to emphasize that I am addressing the content standard, I am continuing to strike through the performance standard.

Summary

Remember, any curriculum statement has two parts: a performance standard and a content standard. That is true for the cognitive, affective, and psychomotor domains. This chapter has asked you to dig a little deeper into your understanding of the content standard—the stuff. You have seen that the content standard is different, depending on which domain of curriculum you are teaching. If you are teaching the core curriculum (mathematics, science, ELA/R, social studies), virtually all the curriculum you are teaching is in the cognitive domain: factual knowledge, procedural knowledge, and/or conceptual knowledge. Outside the core, there is a mixture of all three domains. In the next chapter, I invite you to deepen your understanding of the other half of a curriculum statement: the performance standard.

Descriptors from Texas Teacher Evaluation and Support System (T-TESS) Related to Curriculum Planning

Most teacher evaluation systems express some expectation about your use of the curriculum. Obviously, you want to know and follow your district's expectations. As you analyze the curriculum, ask yourself these questions:

1. Are the curriculum objectives in the cognitive, affective, and/or psychomotor domains? How will this knowledge affect my planning?

2. Am I already thinking about activities that are fully aligned with the state goals and curriculum content standards?

3. How can I integrate academic content from other curriculum areas so that students recognize the connectivity across disciplines?

4. How can I design a lesson so that students are doing a variety of deep, complex thinking?

5. How can I design the lesson in ways that connect to the prior knowledge, experiences, and skills of the diversity of students in my classroom?

From the T-TESS Scoring Guide

<u>Standards and Alignment</u>

Dimension 1.1: The teacher designs clear, well-organized, sequential lessons that reflect best practice, align with standards and are appropriate for diverse learners.

- All goals aligned to state content standards.

- All activities, materials and assessments that:

    ◦ are relevant to students

    ◦ provide appropriate time for lesson and lesson closure

    ◦ fit into the broader unit and course objectives

    ◦ are appropriate for diverse learners

- All objectives aligned to the lesson's goal.

- Integration of technology when applicable. Dimension

    ◦ All goals aligned to state content standards.

    ◦ All objectives aligned to the lesson's goal.

<u>Knowledge of Students</u>

PLANNING DIMENSION 1.3: Through knowledge of students and proven practices, the teacher ensures high levels of learning, social-emotional development and achievement for all students.

- All lessons that connect to students' prior knowledge and experiences.

- Adjustments to address strengths and gaps in background knowledge, life experiences and skills of all students

<u>Content Knowledge and Expertise</u>

Dimension 2.2: The teacher uses content and pedagogical expertise to design and execute lessons aligned with state standards, related content and student needs.

- Conveys accurate content knowledge in multiple contexts.

- Integrates learning objectives with other disciplines.

Works Referenced

Anderson, L. W., et al. (2010). *A taxonomy for learning, teaching, and assessing: A revision of Bloom's taxonomy of educational objectives*. New York: Longman.

Bloom, Benjamin S., et al. (1956). *The taxonomy of educational objectives: the classification of educational goals, handbook I: cognitive domain*. New York: David McKay Company, Inc.

Clark, D.R. (2004). *Bloom's taxonomy: The affective domain*. Retrieved from http://www.nwlink.com/~donclark/hrd/Bloom/affective_domain.html

Crafton Hills College (1995). *SLOs, Bloom's taxonomy, cognitive, psychomotor, and affective domains*. Retrieved from https://www.craftonhills.edu/~/media/Files/SBCCD/CHC/Faculty%20and%20Staff/SLOs/Step%201/Blooms%20Taxonomy%20and%203%20Domains%20of%20Learning.pdf

Kelly, J. (2016). *Psychomotor domain*. Peak Performance Center. Retrieved from http://thepeakperformancecenter.com/educational-learning/learning/process/domains-of-learning/psychomotor-domain/

Simpson E.J. (1972). *The classification of educational objectives in the psychomotor domain*. Washington, DC: Gryphon House.

Texas Education Agency (2016). *Texas teacher evaluation and support system: T-TESS appraiser handbook*. Austin, TX.

Texas Education Code - EDUC § 39.0236.

Wilson, L. O. (2018). *The second principal*. Retrieved from http://thesecondprinciple.com/instructional-design/threedomainsoflearning/

CHAPTER 3

CURRICULUM PERFORMANCE STANDARD

Recall from Chapter 1 that curriculum standards have two components: a performance standard and a content standard (the stuff). In Chapter 2, I defined and gave examples of content standards. This chapter will address the performance standard.

What Are Performance Standards?

The performance standard is what you want students to <u>do</u> with the content standard (the stuff). If you use the traditional Bloom's Taxonomy of Cognitive Learning, the performance standard communicates the complexity or sophistication with which you want students to do something with the content knowledge. Does the curriculum performance call for the students to Know, Understand, Analyze, Evaluate, and/or Create the content knowledge? The performance standard always includes an action verb (e.g., list, summarize, analyze, choose, etc.). These actions are measurable. Performance standards such as *know, understand,* etc. are not measurable. How do you know if your students know? How do you know that they understand? Your students must <u>do</u> something; then you know if they *know* or *understand.* This is the reason that well-written curriculum objective are called "behavioral objectives"—they can be measured through some kind of student behavior. The behavior should be whatever behavior the performance standards (verb) prescribe.

Why Are the Performance Standards Important?

Depth and Complexity (Rigor) of Learning

You want your teaching to result in student learning that has depth, complexity, and connectivity. A synonym for depth and complexity that you may find in the education literature is the word *rigor*. The <u>minimum</u> depth and complexity of the learning is determined by the performance standard. Wanting the students to *list* the content does not have the depth and complexity of wanting them to *analyze* the content. The depth/complexity/rigor of learning is <u>not</u> in the content standard; it's in the performance standard—what you want the students to <u>do</u> with the content/stuff.

<u>Remember that every curriculum statement begins with the phrase, "The student is expected to…."</u> What they are expected to do is "verb some stuff." The performance standard is not about what <u>you as the teacher</u> are expected to do—it's about what the <u>students</u> are expected to be able do. Before you plan a lesson, it is therefore critical that you understand what your students are expected to do by the end of the lesson.

State Assessment

The state assessments in Texas have all been *criterion-referenced* tests. The "criteria" that are tested are the state curriculum standards--Texas Essential Knowledge and Skills (TEKS). Over their 35+ year history, the tests have progressively become more rigorous:

- 1980: Texas Assessment of Basic Skills (TABS)

- 1986 Texas Educational Assessment of Minimum Skills (TEAMS)

- 1990 Texas Assessment of Academic Skills (TAAS)

- 2003 The Texas Assessment of Knowledge and Skills (TAKS)

- 2011 State of Texas Assessment of Academic Readiness (STAAR)

In each iteration of state assessment, the degree of depth and complexity has increased. In 1980, the TABS test assessed "basic skills"—a rather low-level test. Every subsequent assessment required students to demonstrate their learning at higher levels. You may have heard comments from other teachers such as, "The STAAR is so much harder." They are correct. TAAS and TAKS tested the content standard but frequently tested below the level of the performance standard. The factor that makes STAAR *harder* is that, for the first time, the state is assessing the content at the level of the performance standard. Later in this chapter, I will make the case that virtually none of the TEKS have performance standards at the Know or Understand levels. They are almost all at the Apply and Analyze level. The increased rigor of the STAAR lies in the performance standard, not the content standard.

Law and Policy

Remember, state law and your local school board policy require that you teach the curriculum (the TEKS as defined by your school district). While that requirement includes the content standard of the curriculum, it also includes the performance standard. Your students must not only learn the academic content, but you must design the instruction in such a way that all students are learning that content at at least the level of the performance standard— <u>verbing</u> the stuff.

Performance Standards in Cognitive Curriculum

As I pointed out in Chapter 2, almost all of the core curriculum is in the Cognitive Domain. Loosely defined, cognition is "acquiring and processing content knowledge." Students acquire content knowledge and then "process" it. Those processes are generally defined in the context of Bloom's Taxonomy of Cognitive Learning as Know, Understand, Apply, Analyze, Evaluate, Create. The most common contemporary visual model is depicted as a pyramid.

Taxonomy of Cognitive Learning

Figure 1

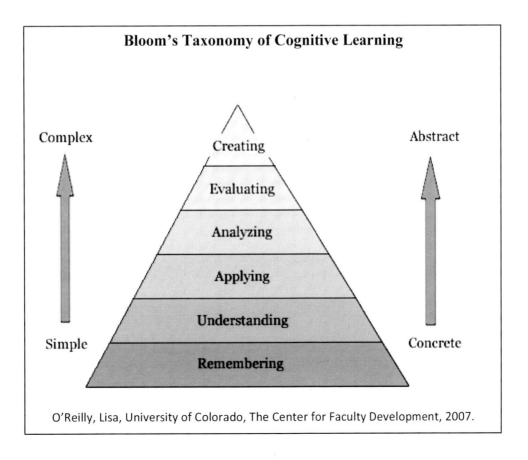

O'Reilly, Lisa, University of Colorado, The Center for Faculty Development, 2007.

I believe a better mental model for this taxonomy is a stair-stepped model, not the pyramidal model that you frequently see. I'll explain my reasoning in a bit.

Figure 2

Bloom's Taxonomy of Cognitive Learning					
					Create
				Evaluate	Evaluate
			Analyze	Analyze	Analyze
		Apply	Apply	Apply	Apply
	Understand	Understand	Understand	Understand	Understand
Remember	Remember	Remember	Remember	Remember	Remember

The following is a brief description of what each level requires in terms of student thinking:

Remember

In the original Bloom's Taxonomy of Cognitive Learning, this "level" was called Knowledge. Unfortunately, this was understood as retrieving information from short-term memory. Anderson *et.al.* correctly define Remembering as "…retrieving knowledge from <u>long-term memory</u> that is consistent with the presented information…." If the student cannot retrieve knowledge from long-term memory, the student never really <u>knew</u> it—the student just memorized it for purposes of short-term memory in order to regurgitate it on some teacher assessment. Two weeks later, the knowledge was gone; so the student really did not <u>learn</u> it. Anderson, *et.al.* explain the phenomenon this way:

"Where teachers concentrate solely on rote learning, teaching, and assessing, (they) focus solely on remembering elements or fragments of knowledge, often in isolation from their context. When teachers focus on meaningful learning, however, remembering knowledge is integrated within the larger task of constructing new knowledge or solving new problems."

In other words, unless students are asked to do something (apply, analyze, etc.) with the knowledge, the time spent memorizing and regurgitating knowledge is in vain. Interestingly, after the primary grade levels, almost all the performance standards in the core curriculum are at the apply/analyze levels. Virtually none ask students to simply recall knowledge. Some examples of Remember performances include: recalling important dates and events; spelling a word correctly; defining a word the way it was defined by the teacher or textbook.

Understand

In the original Bloom's Taxonomy of Cognitive Learning, this "level" was called Comprehension. According to Anderson, *et.al.*, "The Bible" on Bloom's Taxonomy of Cognitive Learning, Understand is defined as "constructing meaning from instructional messages, including oral, written, and graphic communication." My experience tells me that, in practice, Anderson, *et.al.'s* definitions and examples are much more complex than they should be. Many of their examples, I believe, fit better with the Analyze level of the taxonomy. At the Remember level, students basically gave back information in the same way it was given; they may or may not understand what they are saying. At the Understand level, students should be able to explain, summarize, or draw/sketch/manipulate something in a way that says they really understand.

Some examples of Understand performances include: explain the knowledge in your own words, draw a picture of the knowledge; and/or write a short summary. Again, beyond the primary grades there are very few performance standards in the core curriculum that are written at the Understand level.

Apply

In the original Bloom's Taxonomy of Cognitive Learning, this "level" was called Application. Apply has at least two dimensions of understanding: applying procedural knowledge and applying conceptual knowledge.

When applying procedural knowledge (following steps/rules), a student completes a procedure associated with a task. The task is usually a familiar one and provides clues as to the appropriate procedure to use. One of my colleagues, Jane Silvey, refers to this task as "routinized application." For example, in mathematics many worksheets and textbook exercises ask students to use a specific algorithm. There are 10 whole number problems on a worksheet or textbook exercise that require students "work the problem" that is already set up in the algorithmic format. Anderson refers to this application of procedural knowledge as "executing."

When applying conceptual knowledge, the students are confronted with a problem, but it is one in which they have no clues as to what procedures to use. They must understand what the problem is asking, look in their tool kit, and determine what tool(s) are necessary to solve the problem. As one teacher told me, "The students know <u>how</u> to divide, but they don't know <u>when</u> to divide." In other words, students know the algorithms out of context, but they cannot read a problem and determine which of the many algorithms to use. This ability requires a conceptual understanding rather than merely a procedural understanding of all the algorithms.

English Language Arts teachers see this with disturbing regularity. Students know the rules for subject/verb agreement. They do well on the subject/verb agreement exercises/ worksheets. However, when they write, they are unable to apply that knowledge—it's as if they never heard of subject/verb agreement! Grrrr! They know the rule and can apply it out of context (procedural learning). However, when they are required to apply the procedural knowledge within a new and unfamiliar context (e.g., their own writing), there is frequently no transfer of the learning.

Analyze

In the original Bloom's Taxonomy of Cognitive Learning, this "level" was called Analysis. Turning, as always, to Anderson, *et. al.*, "Analysis involves breaking material (*concepts and procedures*) into its constituent parts and determining how the parts are related to one another and to an overall structure." When the definition refers to constituent parts, it really means that you are taking the concept or procedure apart in order to know its critical attributes. Madeline Hunter offered us two related definitions of critical attributes:

1. Critical attributes are those traits/characteristics of the knowledge (conceptual or procedural) that never change.

2. Critical attributes are those traits/characteristics of the knowledge (conceptual or procedural) that make it unique and different from other knowledge.

Let's apply those definitions to an easy concept: mammal. What are the traits/ characteristics of a mammal that never change? What are the traits/characteristics of a mammal that make it unique and different from other living things? The National Wildlife Federation would answer:

*   All mammals have hair.

*   All mammals have a backbone. They are vertebrates.

*   All mammals are warm-blooded.

*   All female mammals produce milk to nourish their young.

*   All mammals give live birth.

In other words, any living thing that has this <u>set</u> of characteristics is a mammal. Any living thing that that does not have this <u>set</u> of characteristics is <u>not</u> a mammal. According to biologists Wilson and Reeder, there are more than 5,000 mammals in the world; all 5,000 have these five critical attributes!

When you are teaching <u>procedural knowledge</u>, the critical attributes are steps and/or rules. For example, in English grammar, a singular subject must have a singular verb—ALWAYS. In procedural mathematics, these steps/rules are commonly referred to as algorithms: "a procedure for solving a mathematical problem (as of finding the greatest <u>common divisor</u>) in a finite number of steps that frequently involves repetition of an operation; a step-by-step procedure for solving a problem or accomplishing some end." (Merriam Webster)

So, what does this have to do with anything? At the analysis level, you are planning lessons in which students identify the critical attributes of the concept or procedure. This is the essential learning. For example, the analysis processes below require that students <u>first</u> know the critical attributes:

Classify: All classification system are based on critical attributes. The classification "mammal" requires that any living thing in that classification have hair, have a backbone, be warm-blooded, produce milk to nourish its young, and give live birth. The classification "quadrilateral" means that the figure has four sides—no exceptions.

Compare: You cannot compare two "wholes." You cannot meaningfully compare two short stories. You can, however, compare them if you know the critical attributes of <u>any</u> short story: plot structure, setting, theme (sometimes), conflict, characters, and author's perspective/point of view. While you cannot compare the short stories as a whole, you can compare their plot structures, their settings, their characters, etc. You must know the critical attributes of the concept before you can meaningfully compare or contrast.

As you will see when you read the definitions of *Evaluate* (evaluation) and *Create* (synthesis), you will see that the so-called "higher-level" thinking processes are dependent on knowing the critical attributes of the concept or procedure. This dependence reinforces my representation of the cognitive domain as a stair-step model (Figure 2).

Evaluate

In the original Bloom's Taxonomy of Cognitive Learning, this "level" was called Evaluation and was the highest level of the taxonomy. Our old friends Anderson, *et. al.* define Evaluate as making "judgments based on criteria and standards." The specific evaluation could be critiquing, choosing best alternatives, deciding between/among alternatives, or debating. Notice the definition contains the phrase "based on criteria and standards." It is <u>not</u> just what the student thinks/believes; remember, this is <u>cognitive learning</u>, NOT <u>affective</u> learning. For example, in government class student might be asked to critique our current system of health care delivery. The "criteria and standards" would include (here they come again!) the critical attributes of <u>any</u> health care system, such as cost, who pays, outcomes, accessibility, coverage, source of health care decisions, etc. Those critical attributes would be the "criteria and standards" for critiquing the current health care system.

When the performance standard is at the evaluation level, there are always two verbs—if the curriculum is accurately written.

Figure 3

Evaluate		Defend
Critique		Support
Choose	**AND**	Prove
Decide		Justify
Debate		Make a case for…
		using the agreed upon criteria and standards

The real cognition is in the second verb (defend, support, etc.). You may, appropriately, decide that whatever the students do in the left column is "correct" (there may be exceptions when the response is racist, sexist, etc.). Your full assessment comes from the second verb. No matter what the student "decides/chooses," he/she <u>must</u> defend/support/justify the choice based on the agreed upon criteria and standards. It's not just their opinion. That might be acceptable with affective learning; it is not acceptable with cognitive learning.

Create

In the original Bloom's Taxonomy of Cognitive Learning, this "level" was called Synthesis. Back to Anderson, *et. al.*—they are, after all, the premier experts! They define Create as "put(ting) elements together to form a coherent or functional whole; reorganize elements into a new pattern or structure." Notice the word "elements" in their definition. Instead of elements, think "critical attributes." At the Create level, the student is taking the critical attributes of the original and monkeying around with them to create something different. The performance standard may ask them to do things such as change, create, combine, or speculate ("What if…?").

Let's take the health care system example from the previous section on Evaluate. After students have evaluated the current health care system (using the standards and criteria), they are asked to create an ideal health care system. That would inevitably lead them to change or modify one or more of the critical attributes: cost, who pays, outcomes, accessibility, coverage, source of health care decisions, etc. When they are finished, they will have "created" a new health care system because they changed/modified one or more of the critical attributes.

Speculation has great potential in driving the Create level:

- If George Washington had lost Yorktown, what would the next ten years of American history have looked like? (The question proposed changing a critical attribute of that period and creates a new and different period of history.)

- If a gene in a particular seed were externally engineered to behave differently, what would be the impact on crop production? (By changing the genetic makeup of the seed, you would have created a new seed, maybe one that is more drought resistant or yields more plants per acre.)

Just as in Evaluate, when the performance standard is at the Create level, there are always two verbs—if the curriculum is accurately written.

Figure 4

Change		Defend
Create		Support
Combine	**AND**	Prove
Invent		Justify
Devise a procedure for…		Make a case for…
Generate an alternative hypothesis		*using the agreed upon criteria and standards*
Speculate ("What if…?")		

Repeating what I said in the section on Evaluate, the real cognition is in the second verb (defend, support, etc.). You may, appropriately, decide that whatever the student does in the left column is "correct" (there may be exceptions when the response is racist, sexist, etc.). Your full assessment comes from the second verb. No matter what the student "creates," he/she <u>must</u> defend/support/justify the creation based on the agreed upon criteria and standards.

Before leaving cognitive learning, let me point out some misunderstandings and some assumptions about Bloom's Taxonomy of Cognitive Learning.

Most Common Misunderstanding About the Verbs

THE VERBS ARE NOT MAGIC—THEY LIVE IN A CONTEXT

The verbs are not magic. When you look at a traditional "Bloom's Verb Chart," the chart has verbs organized around the six levels of Bloom's Taxonomy of Cognitive Learning. These charts can be very misleading. The level of complexity is not in the verb alone. The verb lives in a context; some verbs could actually be at any one of the six levels, depending on that context. Verbs such as *identify* and *describe* are generally associated with the Know and Understand levels of complexity of the taxonomy. But let's put those verbs into some different contexts.

- <u>Identify</u> the capitals of the fifty states in the United States. This is low-level (<u>Know</u>) learning.

- <u>Identify</u> the similarities and differences between…. When students are looking at similarities/differences (compare/contrast), they must know the critical attributes of the two things being compared/contrasted. This is <u>Analyze</u> level thinking.

- <u>Identify</u> the strengths and weaknesses of… and justify your thinking. This is <u>Evaluate</u> level thinking.

- <u>Identify</u> ways to change this piece of writing so that the reader is better able to "see" what is happening and justify the recommendations. This is true editorial revision and is at the <u>Create</u> level.

It's the same verb: identify. But the verb has no meaning in isolation—it must be viewed in the context of the curriculum statement. "Identify" could be at any level of the taxonomy, depending on what the student is asked to identify.

Figure 5

Bloom's Taxonomy of Cognitive Learning					
					Create
				Evaluate	Evaluate
			Analyze	Analyze	Analyze
		Apply	Apply	Apply	Apply
	Understand	Understand	Understand	Understand	Understand
Remember	Remember	Remember	Remember	Remember	Remember

It is interesting to note how much of our common education language comes from this stair-step model:

- Higher level questions and tasks

- Low level questions and tasks

- "Bump it up"

- More complex thinking/problem solving

Earlier in this chapter, I indicated that the "stair-step" mental model is more instructive than the pyramid models that you frequently find. Here's why.

First Assumption: Bloom's is Cumulative.

Remember, that classification systems (like this cognitive one) are based on critical attributes. The chief critical attribute of Bloom's Taxonomy of Cognitive Learning is <u>complexity.</u> As thinking moves "up" the taxonomy, the thinking becomes more complex. That is because each level carries the previous level with it.

- In order to Understand, students have to Remember—they are doing two things at the same time.

- In order to Analyze, students have to Remember, Understand, and Apply—they are doing four things at the same time.

- In order to Create, they have to Remember, Understand, Apply, Analyze, and Evaluate—they are doing six things at the same time!

The performance standard in most curriculum objectives in the Texas Essential Knowledge and Skills (TEKS) is written at the application or (mostly) analysis level. That does not necessarily mean that students learning starts at the Analyze level. If the performance standard is at the Analyze level, they typically also need to Know, Understand, and Apply. The curriculum outcome may be written at the Analyze level, but the learning may need to start at the Know level in order to reach that analysis outcome.

Second Assumption: Bloom's is Sequential for Deductive Learning.

Conventional wisdom has generally been that learning must start at the bottom of the taxonomy (Know) and progressively build up through Understand, Apply, Analyze, etc. That belief is accurate if the <u>learning model/lesson design</u> is deductive. In other words, if the lesson design is teacher-centered and the students will receive all the information in the content standard (the stuff) from the teacher, the lesson will begin the thinking/learning at the bottom and work up. While I will have more to say about deductive learning in Chapter 5, here's a simple way to think about a deductive lesson. (I am grateful to my longtime friend and colleague, Ron Simpson, for this mental model.)

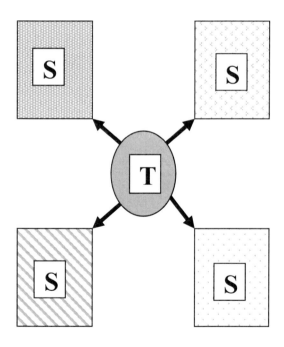

Texas Education Agency (1991)
Alternative Models of Instruction.
Austin, TX. (Visual by Ron Simpson)

The mental model on the left represents a **deductive lesson**. The teacher is the center of attention, and all/most of the knowledge (stuff) comes from the teacher (illustrated by the arrows going from the teacher to the students). In this model, students are generally passive recipients of the stuff. There may be varying degrees of interaction between the teacher and individual students.

If this is the lesson design, student learning will typically begin at Know and progress sequentially "up" the taxonomy as far as the teacher has planned for them to go. Remember that most performance standards are written at the Apply/Analyze levels, so the teacher must plan for all students to reach those levels of thinking. One problem with the deductive model is time. When you start off with the foundation content, you can easily run out of time before you get the students to the Apply/Analyze levels.

Third Assumption: Bloom's Is Not Necessarily Sequential in Inductive Learning.

With an inductive <u>learning model/lesson</u>, student learning/thinking does not necessarily begin at the bottom (Know) and build up. In fact, an inductive lesson will probably begin at the Analyze level and build down. This model has had many names: constructivist, inquiry, discovery, etc. By whatever name, these are all inductive models of thinking/learning.

Once again, I (with Ron Simpson's assistance) offer a simple way to think about inductive learning:

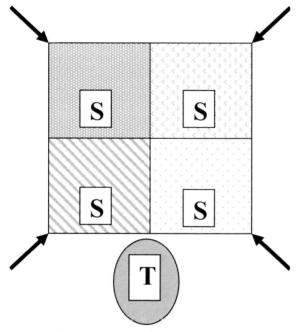

Texas Education Agency (1991)
Alternative Models of Instruction.
Austin, TX. (Visual by Ron Simpson)

The mental model on the left represents an **inductive lesson**. The teacher has carefully designed a series of tasks though which all/most of the knowledge (stuff) is obtained by the students (illustrated by the arrows NOT going from the teacher to the students). In this model, students are generally active participants in the learning. They, not the teacher, are doing the work and the thinking. The "stuff" may come from their schema (prior experience/learning), from research, from investigation/experimentation, from each other, etc. For this process to be successful, most of the teacher's work is done before arriving in the classroom. There must be sufficient structure, resources, and parameters within which the student will successfully acquire the knowledge (stuff) that, in the deductive model, would have come from the teacher.

If this is the lesson design, student learning will typically begin at the Analyze level and progress back down the taxonomy to construct and organize the Know and Understand levels.

The teacher's role is to monitor and interact with students, challenge and extend their thinking, and correct and redirect when they are having difficulty. I think of this model as a way to wander around and mess with their heads as they become the center of the learning. That's the fun of teaching!!

Performance Standards in Affective and Psychomotor Curriculum

Up to this point, I have addressed performance standards in the <u>cognitive domain</u>. The performance standards set an outcome for the level of student thinking—what they are supposed to <u>do</u> with content standard (stuff). Remember that if you are teaching in the core curriculum (mathematics, science, social studies, English Language Arts/Reading), almost all your curriculum is in the cognitive domain.

In Chapter 2, I introduced you to two other domains of curriculum: the affective and the psychomotor. If you teach outside the core in areas such as CTE, the visual and performing arts, health and physical education, etc., you also have curriculum standards in the cognitive domain. However, unlike the core, much of your curriculum is in the affective and psychomotor domains. In these two domains, the performance standards are very different from the performance standards in the cognitive domain. The most complex learning in the affective domain (called Characterizing by Value) implies that the belief/value is so much a part of who you are that you instinctively make decisions based on that value. Fortunately, we have taxonomies to guide our understanding of the differences in the performances among these three domains.

Taxonomy of Performances in the Affective Domain

Thankfully, Brother Bloom has provided us with a second taxonomy—this one of affective learning. Like the taxonomy of cognitive learning, it speaks to the performance standard (the verb in its context)—what the students are expected to <u>do</u> with the content standard (stuff).

Remember that affective curriculum is <u>not</u> the incidental teaching of things such as hard work, honesty, respect, etc. Affective curriculum is very overt and intentional. The curriculum determines what values, attitudes, beliefs, etc. you should have. If you think of religious education, its intent is frequently to overtly teach the values and beliefs of a particular faith and to hold and act on them.

Figure 6

| | | | | Bloom's Taxonomy of Affective Learning |

				Characterizing by Value or Value Concept
			Organizing and Conceptualizing	Organizing and Conceptualizing
		Valuing	Valuing	Valuing
	Responding	Responding	Responding	Responding
Receiving	Receiving	Receiving	Receiving	Receiving

Note at least two similarities between both the affective and cognitive taxonomies.

1. They both progress "up" because of the <u>complexity</u> of the learner's thinking and action.

2. They are both <u>cumulative</u>. When your actions are at the top of the taxonomy (Characterizing by Value), you are at the same time Organizing and Conceptualizing, Valuing, Responding, and Receiving.

The following chart provides a brief (and over simplified) explanation of each level.

Figure 7

Category
Receiving: Awareness of the value/belief; willingness to hear it; understands the value/belief.
Responding: Reacts to a particular belief/value; there is a willingness to respond or satisfaction in responding (motivation) to the belief/value.
Valuing: Attaches worth to a belief/value; ranges from simple acceptance to the more complex state of commitment. Valuing is based on the internalization of a set of specified values, while clues to these beliefs/values are expressed in the learner's overt behavior and are often identifiable.
Organizing and Conceptualizing: Organizes beliefs/values into priorities by contrasting different values, resolving conflicts between them, and creating a unique value system. The emphasis is on comparing, relating, and synthesizing values.
Characterization by Value or Value Concept: Has a value system that controls their behavior. The behavior is pervasive, consistent, predictable, and most important characteristic of the learner. The learner instinctively and intuitively makes life choices based on the belief/value.

*Adapted from Kelly, James (2016) **Affective domain**. Peak Performance Center.*

Recall some of the examples of affective curriculum from Chapter 2. The students is expected to:

- compare and contrast animal rights and animal welfare (Texas Essential Knowledge and Skills: Small Animal Management). [Commentary: The content standard clearly asks students to make value judgements about animal rights and welfare—the fourth level of complexity of the taxonomy, Organizing and Conceptualizing.]

- explain the characteristics of personal values and principles (Texas Essential Knowledge and Skills: Culinary Arts). [Commentary: Again, the content standard involves defining and explaining "personal values and principles"—the second level of the taxonomy, Responding.]

- identify and describe strategies for avoiding drugs, violence, gangs, weapons, and other harmful situations (Texas Essential Knowledge and Skills: 6th Grade Health). [Commentary: The content standard calls on students to develop strategies for avoiding drugs, violence, weapons, and other harmful situations—the second level of complexity of the taxonomy, Responding.]

Don't forget that affective learning also includes an element of cognitive learning. In the previous examples, students must have cognitive knowledge of animal rights and welfare, personal values and principles, and the nature and prevalence of drugs/violence/weapons/other harmful situations. The difference here is that the emphasis is not primarily on the cognitive knowledge of the curriculum—the emphasis is on beliefs, values, and actions surrounding that knowledge.

Taxonomy of Performance Standards in the Psychomotor Domain

In Chapter 2, I pointed out that the content standards (stuff) may include such physical skills as movement, coordination, manipulation, dexterity, grace, strength, etc. Wilson defines psychomotor learning as "specific to discreet physical functions, reflex actions and interpretive movements." Traditionally, these types of objectives are concerned with physically encoding information, with movement and/or with activities where the gross and fine muscles are used for expressing or interpreting information or concepts. This area also refers to natural, autonomic responses or reflexes.

Note, again, the similarities among the taxonomies of all three domains.

1. They all progress "up" because of the <u>complexity</u> of the learner's thinking and action.

2. They are both cumulative. When your actions are at the top of the taxonomy (Naturalization), you are at the same time Articulating, moving with Precision, etc.

Clearly, performance standards in the psychomotor domain are physical performances (in athletics, dance, playing a musical instrument, etc.) using muscles, hands, arms, legs, lips, diaphragm, tongue, etc. While Brother Bloom has not provided us with a taxonomy of psychomotor learning, there are several that have been developed by others. One that I find helpful was developed by Dave, Harrow, Simpson, and Grouland. Like the taxonomy of cognitive learning, this one also speaks to the performance standard (the verb in its context)— what the students are expected to <u>do</u> with the content standard (stuff).

Figure 8

Taxonomy of Psychomotor Learning

Dave, Harrow, Simpson, Gronlund, and others (2005). School of Education, University of Mississippi.

				Naturalization
			Articulation	Articulation
		Precision	Precision	Precision
	Manipulation	Manipulation	Manipulation	Manipulation
Imitation	Imitation	Imitation	Imitation	Imitation

The following chart from the authors provides a brief (and over-simplified) explanation of each level.

Figure 9

Level	Definition
Imitate	The ability to observe and pattern your behavior after someone else. At this level, you simply copy someone else or replicate someone's actions following observations.
Manipulate	The ability to perform certain actions by memory or by following instructions. At this level, you can perform a task from written or verbal instructions.
Precision	The ability to perform certain actions with some level of expertise and without help or intervention from others. At this level, you are able to perform a skill with a high degree of precision and accuracy and with few errors.
Articulation	The ability to adapt and integrate multiple actions that develop methods to meet varying and novel requirements. At this level, your skills are so well developed that you can modify movement to fit special requirements or to meet a problem situation.
Naturalization	The ability to perform actions in an automatic, intuitive, or unconscious way. At this level, your performance is automatic with little physical or mental exertion. Your performance has become second-nature or natural, without needing to think much about it.

*Adapted from Kelly, James (2016) **Psychomotor domain**. Peak Performance Center.*

Once again, don't forget that psychomotor learning also includes an element of cognitive learning. In music education, for example, a student would generally be expected to read musical notes (cognitive learning) as a part of learning to play a musical instrument. The difference here is that the emphasis is not primarily on the cognitive knowledge of the curriculum (e.g., verbally describe how to serve a volleyball)—the emphasis is a physical performance surrounding that knowledge (actually serving a volleyball).

Summary

Curriculum is not just content (stuff). What students will do with the stuff is critical to long-term retention and transfer of the stuff. In determining what the students will do, consider what I have presented in this chapter:

1. Know which domain of curriculum you are teaching: cognitive, affective, or psychomotor.

2. Understand which level of complexity or sophistication the curriculum expects students to demonstrate their knowledge or skill. Generally, most curriculum objectives are written at the higher levels of complexity. If they are written at low levels, what would be the point in students spending time acquiring knowledge or skills that they never use? And if they never use them, they will not retain them.

3. Affective and psychomotor learning will always have some elements of cognitive learning.

4. You must analyze the curriculum and then plan the instruction that assures that students are

    a. acquiring the knowledge and skill specified in the curriculum and

    b. operating with that knowledge/skill at at least the level of the curriculum's performance standard.

As you plan the learning for students, there must be one or more activities/tasks in which ALL of the students are verbing the stuff.

Question for Planning

Most teacher evaluation systems express some expectation about your use of the curriculum. Obviously, you want to know and follow your district's expectations. As you analyze the curriculum, especially the performance standards, ask yourself these questions:

1. Are the curriculum objectives in the cognitive, affective, and/or psychomotor domains? How will this knowledge affect my planning?

2. What might it look like/sound like if all my students are operating at the level of the performance standards? What can I plan for them to do so that all of them are "verbing the stuff?"

3. Am I already thinking about activities that are fully aligned with the performance standard of the state curriculum?

4. How can I design the lesson so that students are doing a variety of deep, complex thinking or activity?

5. How can I design the lesson in ways that connect to the prior knowledge, experiences, and skills of the diversity of students in my classroom?

Descriptors from Texas Teacher Evaluation and Support System (T-TESS) Related to Curriculum Planning and Instruction

<u>Standards and Alignment</u>

Dimension 1.1: The teacher designs clear, well-organized, sequential lessons that reflect best practice, align with standards and are appropriate for diverse learners.

- All goals aligned to state content standards.

- All activities, materials and assessments that:

    ◦ are relevant to students

    ◦ provide appropriate time for lesson and lesson closure

    ◦ fit into the broader unit and course objectives

    ◦ are appropriate for diverse learners

- All objectives aligned to the lesson's goal.

- Integration of technology when applicable.

- All goals aligned to state content standards.

- All objectives aligned to the lesson's goal.

From the T-TESS Scoring Guide

Knowledge of Students

PLANNING DIMENSION 1.3: Through knowledge of students and proven practices, the teacher ensures high levels of learning, social-emotional development and achievement for all students.

- All lessons that connect to students' prior knowledge and experiences.

- Adjustments to address strengths and gaps in background knowledge, life experiences and skills of all students

Content Knowledge and Expertise

Dimension 2.2: The teacher uses content and pedagogical expertise to design and execute lessons aligned with state standards, related content and student needs.

- Conveys accurate content knowledge in multiple contexts.

- Integrates learning objectives with other disciplines.

Works Referenced

Anderson, Lorin W., Krathwohl, Airasian, Peter W., and Cruikshank, Kathleen A., Mayer, Richard E., Pintrich, Paul, R., Raths, James, Wittrock, Merlin C. (2010). A taxonomy for learning, teaching, and assessing: A revision of Bloom's taxonomy of educational objectives. New York: Longman.

Bloom, Benjamin S., Ebglehart, Max D., Furst, Edward J., Hill, Walker H, and Krathwohl, (1956). The taxonomy of educational objectives, the classification of educational goals, Handbook I: Cognitive domain. New York: David McKay Company, Inc.

Clark, D.R. (2004). *Bloom's taxonomy: The affective domain.* Retrieved from http://www. nwlink.com/~donclark/hrd/Bloom/affective_domain.html

Crafton Hills College. "SLOs, Bloom's Taxonomy, Cognitive, Psychomotor, and Affective Domains".Retrieved from https://www.craftonhills.edu/~/media/Files/SBCCD/CHC/ Faculty%20and%20Staff/SLOs/Step%201/Blooms%20Taxonomy%20and%203%20 Domains%20of%20Learning.pdf

Hunter, Madeine (1971). Teach for transfer. El Segundo, CA: TIP Publications

Kelly, James (2016, February 16). Psychomotor domain. Peak Performance Center. Retrieved from http://thepeakperformancecenter.com/educational-learning/learning/process/domains-of-learning/psychomotor-domain/

Merriam-Webster On-Line Dictionary (2017). Retrieved at https://www.merriam-webster.com/dictionary/algorithm

Natural History Museum of Los Angeles, California (2017). *Mammalian FAQs:* Los Angeles California. Retrieved from https://nhm.org/site/research-collections/mammalogy/faqs

National Wildlife Federation, *Mammals* (2017. Retrieved from https://www.nwf.org/Wildlife/Wildlife-Library/Mammals.aspx

O'Reilly, Lisa, University of Colorado, The Center for Faculty Development, 2007. Retrieved from http://www.ucdenver.edu/faculty_staff/faculty/center-for-faculty-development/Documents/Tutorials/Assessment/module2/index.htm

The Second Principal. Wilson, Leslie Owen. Retrieved from http://thesecondprinciple.com/instructional-design/threedomainsoflearning/

Simpson E.J. (1972). *The Classification of Educational Objectives in the Psychomotor Domain.* Washington, DC: Gryphon House.

National Wildlife Federation (2017). *Mammals:* Merrifield, VA. https://www.nwf.org/Wildlife/Wildlife-Library/Mammals.aspx

Natural History Museum of Los Angeles, California (2017). *Mammalian FAQs:* Los Angeles California.

Retrieved from: https://nhm.org/site/research-collections/mammalogy/faqs

Texas Education Agency (2001), Alternative Models of Instruction, Austin, Texas.

Texas Education Agency (2016). Texas Teacher Evaluation and Support System: T-TESS Appraiser Handbook.

Texas Education Code - EDUC § 39.0236

Wilson, Leslie Owen. The second principal. Retrieved from http://thesecondprinciple.com/instructional-design/threedomainsoflearning/

CHAPTER 4

PLANNING AND ANALYZING THE CURRICULUM

In the first three chapters you learned the two components of the curriculum: a performance standard (verb) and a content standard (stuff). Before you plan exciting and joyful learning for your students, you need to analyze the curriculum standards your students are to learn. This is sometimes referred to as "unpacking" the standards. In brief, that means initially dissecting the content standards (stuff). While this chapter addresses cognitive learning in the four core content areas, the process is generally the same for non-core subjects.

Step 1: Determine what kind of knowledge the content represents. It may be:

Kind of Knowledge	Definition
Conceptual Knowledge	Knowledge of interrelationships among basic elements within a larger structure that enables them to function together.
Procedural Knowledge	Knowledge of how to do something and criteria for using skills, algorithms, techniques, and/or methods.
Factual Knowledge	The basic elements a student must know in order to solve problems and complete tasks; knowledge that is believed to have some value in and of itself.

Ultimately, your decisions about planning the teaching/learning will be very different, depending on what kind a knowledge is to be taught/learned. Teaching a concept requires a very different lesson design than one teaching a procedure. More about that in Chapter 5.

Step 2: If the knowledge (stuff) is conceptual (as almost all of them are), there are THREE things you (and your students) will need to know. This is where the <u>real</u> unpacking begins!

CRITICAL ATTRIBUTES ARE THOSE CHARACTERISTICS (TRAITS, PROPERTIES) OF THE CONCEPT THAT **<u>NEVER CHANGE.</u>**

CRITICAL ATTRIBUTES ARE THOSE CHARACTERISTICS (TRAITS, PROPERTIES) OF THE CONCEPT THAT **<u>MAKE IT UNIQUE/DIFFERENT FROM OTHER CONCEPTS</u>**.

THE CRITICAL ATTRIBUTES ARE TYPICALLY IN THE FORM OF "ALL (*CONCEPT*) HAVE/ARE _____."

THE SET OF CRITICAL ATTRIBUTES MAY BE THE BEST DEFINITION.

THE DEFINITION MAY OR MAY NOT BE HELPFUL.

THE DEFINITION MAY OR MAY NOT ALSO CONTAIN THE CRITICAL ATTRIBUTES.

SOMETIMES INFORMAL OR VISUAL REPRESENTATIONS OF THE CONCEPT MAY BE HELPFUL.

AN EXAMPLE HAS ALL THE CRITICAL ATTRIBUTES OF THE CONCEPT.

A NON-EXAMPLE IS A NON-EXAMPLE BECAUSE IT DOES NOT HAVE ALL OF THE CRITICAL ATTRIBUTES OF THE CONCEPT (OR HAS ADDITIONAL ATTRIBUTES).

THE POWER OF THE EXAMPLE IS THE "WHY?"

1. What are the critical attributes of the concept? In Chapter 3, I defined critical attributes and attempted to explain how vitally important this issue is. Many concepts will be very abstract to some of your students. One of the best ways of moving them from the abstract to the concrete is by identifying the critical attributes.

Your students may need to do research, explore their own schema (prior knowledge and experience), dialogue with each other to share and combine schemas, conduct observations or experiments, etc.

2. What is the definition of the concept? In many cases, discovering the critical attributes may make this step redundant or even unnecessary. Many times textbook and dictionary definitions may make the concept even more abstract—there are too many words in the definition that are unfamiliar, making the formal definition virtually meaningless. If the set of critical attributes defines the concept, stop there. You may, however, want to work at more informal or operational definitions. Sometimes just finding a picture, model, or graphic representation of the concept will create an "ah-hah!" moment.

3. What are some examples and non-examples of the concept? If the student understands the critical attributes of the concept, examples may come intuitively from their schema. But what <u>makes</u> an example an example? The example may be accurate, but <u>why</u> is accurate? This may sound confusing, but try this: an example is an accurate example <u>if it has all critical attributes of the concept</u>. A dog is a mammal because it has all the critical attributes of a mammal. A square, rectangle, rhombus, trapezoid, or parallelogram all look different but they are all quadrilaterals because they all have four-sides with two pairs of parallel and equal sides. Always try to

THE CONCEPT CAN USUALLY BE TAUGHT/LEARNED WITHOUT ADDITIONAL SUBJECT-AREA VOCABULARY/JARGON.

SOME OF THE EXAMPLES MUST BE VISUAL/PICTORIAL.

move beyond verbal examples by finding pictures, models, or graphic representations that are accurate examples of the concept. Don't forget: when you Google the concept, there is a tab at the top of the page for "images"!

You probably have figured out by now that a non-example is something that does not have all of the critical attributes—it is an inaccurate example. A fish is a non-example of a mammal. A triangle is a non-example of a quadrilateral. This is sometimes called backward thinking: determining what something is not rather than what it is. This type of thinking is more complex.

So, when a student gives you an accurate example (or non-example), your next question is "Why?" If the student really understands the concept, the student will be able to explain that the example has all the critical attributes. If the student's example is inaccurate, it is a non-example. This can be just as powerful a learning opportunity as *getting it right* because you can probe and ask questions to help the student discover which critical attributes are missing.

THE CRITICAL ATTRIBUTES OF PROCEDURAL KNOWLEDGE ARE:

- PROCESS STEPS
- RULES

BEHIND THE PROCEDURE LIE CONCEPTS.

YOU SHOULD RARELY, IF EVER, TEACH THE PROCEDURAL KNOWLEDGE WITHOUT FIRST TEACHING THE CONCEPT(S) BEHIND THE PROCEDURE.

Surprise, surprise, you have to know the critical attributes! The critical attributes of procedural knowledge are steps and/or rules. Grammar and punctuation are governed by rules: items in a series must be punctuated by commas; you can debate the Oxford comma on your own time! Laboratory exercises generally follow the process defined in the 8th grade TEKS: design and implement comparative and experimental investigations by making observations, asking well-defined questions, formulating testable hypotheses, and using appropriate equipment and technology. The detailed process may be given to the students by the teacher (typically with a lab sheet for demonstration or deductive learning) or developed by the students (for inductive learning labs).

Remember that (particularly in mathematics) behind the procedural knowledge is conceptual knowledge. Multiplication is a concept. There are also steps and rules for multiplication. If students learn only the procedural knowledge without the conceptual knowledge, it may lead to monkey-see-monkey-do mathematics. Students perform the steps and follow the rules with no conceptual understanding of what they are doing. You should rarely, if ever, teach procedural knowledge without first teaching the concept behind the procedure and ensuring that students have had an opportunity to develop and internalize that concept.

Step 2 (continued): If the knowledge (stuff) is factual, here is what you and your students need to know.

Remember that, with the exception of social studies, there are very few content standards (stuff) that are factual knowledge. But, you say, there is always factual knowledge even if the content standard is conceptual or procedural. And you are, to a degree, correct. Return to my previous examples. Mammal is a concept. Quadrilateral is a concept. When you identify the critical attributes and/or definitions, those attributes/definitions are factual.

Conceptual Content Standard	Factual Knowledge About the Concept
Mammal	1. All mammals have hair. 2. All mammals have a backbone. They are vertebrates. 3. All mammals are warm-blooded. 4. All female mammals produce milk to nourish their young. 5. All mammals give live birth.
Quadrilateral	1. All quadrilaterals have four-sides. 2. All quadrilaterals two pairs of parallel and equal sides.

Don't get so caught up in the factual component that you forget that the emphasis is on the concept! I have heard too many teachers say, "We can't move on until they learn the multiplication table" or "I can't let them write until they learn the grammatical rules, capitalization, and punctuation, etc." This is not true. Students can grasp and apply concepts before they've mastered all the factual knowledge or processes that are associated with it.

I have borrowed some excellent examples of what unpacking the content standard "looks like." You may or may not agree with their specific analysis. However, these examples effectively represent the four core content areas.

COMPLETED FRAYER MODEL: SCIENCE EXAMPLE

Definition	Characteristics
a characteristic of matter that can be seen, felt, heard, smelled, or tasted	• can be measured • describes an object • information that can be obeserved without changing the matter into something else
Examples	Nonexamples
• color • texture • state (solid, liquid, gas) • boiling point • odor	• the way a material behaves in a chemical reaction • chemical properties • can be observed only when one substance changes into a different substance • flammability

Term
physical
property

Frayer Model adapted from Frayer, D.A., Frederick, W.C., & Klausmeier, H.G. (1969). *A schema for testing the level of concept mastery* (Technical report No. 16). Madison, WI: University of Wisconsin Research and Developement Center for Cognitive Learning.

COMPLETED FRAYER MODEL: ENGLISH LANGUAGE ARTS EXAMPLE

Definition	Characteristics
A novel set in the past that contains references to significant events in history. The writer may blend factual information with fictional characters dialogue, details, and events	• Based on historical fact • Set in the past • Set in a real time and place • Some fictional aspects, such as characters, details, or events
Examples	Nonexamples
• Novel about the Civil War • Story about a fictional family during the Great Depression • *Esperanza Rising* by Pam Munoz Ryan • *Number the Stars* by Lois Lowry	• A general's personal account of the events leading to the Iraq War • Story about a family who lives on the moon • *The Lord of the Rings* by J.R.R. Tolkien • *Tuck Everlasting* by Natalie Babbitt

Term
historical
fiction

Frayer Model adapted from Frayer, D.A., Frederick, W.C., & Klausmeier, H.G. (1969). *A schema for testing the level of concept mastery* (Technical report No. 16). Madison, WI: University of Wisconsin Research and Developement Center for Cognitive Learning.

COMPLETED FRAYER MODEL: MATH EXAMPLE

Definition	Characteristics
a polygon with four sides and four angles	• sum of the interior angles = 360 degrees • exactly four sides • exactly four angles • made of line segments • has two diagonals • closed figure
Examples	Nonexamples
• parallelogram • rhombus • square • rectangle • trapezoid	• circle • triangle • oval • straight line • star • octagon

Term
quadrilateral

Frayer Model adapted from Frayer, D.A., Frederick, W.C., & Klausmeier, H.G. (1969). *A schema for testing the level of concept mastery* (Technical report No. 16). Madison, WI: University of Wisconsin Research and Developement Center for Cognitive Learning.

COMPLETED FRAYER MODEL:
SOCIAL STUDIES EXAMPLE

Definition	Characteristics
people moving from one place, region, or country to another	<ul><li>involves a major change (long distance or large group)</li><li>could be forced by natural disaster, economy, warfare</li><li>could be a choice because someone wants a different climate, job, school</li><li>permanent or semi-permanment, not temporary</li></ul>

Term human migration

Examples	Nonexamples
<ul><li>move from Dar el Salam in Tanzania to Zanzibar</li><li>people many years ago walking/floating across the Bering Straigt from Russia to North America</li><li>people moving from rural areas in the southern United States to cities in the North</li></ul>	<ul><li>people staying in one place all their lives</li><li>geese flying from Canada to Mexico</li><li>someone from El Paso, Texas, going to Juarez, Mexico, for the day</li><li>driving from a home in the suburbs to a job in the city</li></ul>

Frayer Model adapted from Frayer, D.A., Frederick, W.C., & Klausmeier, H.G. (1969). *A schema for testing the level of concept mastery* (Technical report No. 16). Madison, WI: University of Wisconsin Research and Developement Center for Cognitive Learning.

Note that I have thus far addressed unpacking the content standard (stuff). To complete the analysis and planning of the curriculum, you still have to unpack the critically important performance standard (verb). That issue will be addressed in the following chapters.

You have now "unpacked" the content standard (stuff). You have a clear and concrete understanding of the content your students are supposed to learn. A separate question that will be addressed later is whether the students acquire this knowledge from you (a deductive process) or you design a series of activities through which your students discover the knowledge (an inductive process).

Summary

1. Before you plan the instruction, you must unpack the curriculum in order to have a concrete understanding of the content standard (stuff).

2. The instructional design will depend on what kind of knowledge the students are expected to learn: conceptual, procedural, or factual.

3. For conceptual knowledge, students must know:
    *   The critical attributes (characteristics, traits, properties, etc.) of the concept.
    *   The definition(s) of the concept, if the critical attributes do not already do that.
    *   Examples and non-examples of the concept and <u>why</u>.

4. For procedural knowledge, students must know:
    *   The critical attributes of the procedure (steps and/or rules).
    *   The critical attributes or the concept on which the procedure is based.

As you analyze the curriculum and begin to think about the instructional activities, ask yourself these questions:

1. If the curriculum objectives are in the cognitive and/or psychomotor domain, do <u>I</u> know:
    *   The critical attributes (characteristics, traits, properties, etc.) of the concept.
    *   The definition(s) of the concept, if the critical attributes do not already do that.
    *   Examples and non-examples of the concept and <u>why.</u>
    *   The critical attributes of the procedure (steps and/or rules).
    *   The critical attributes or the concept on which the procedure is based.

2. What might it look like/sound like if all my students are operating at the level of the performance standards? What can I plan for them to do so that all of them are "verbing the stuff"?

3. How can I design a lesson so that all students are doing a variety of deep, complex thinking?

4. How can I design the lesson in ways that connect to the prior knowledge, experiences, and skills of the diversity of students in my classroom?

5. What questions and/or activities can I plan so that:

    *   all students engage in complex, higher-order thinking.

    *   instructional groups are based on the needs of all students.

    *   all students understand their individual roles within instructional groups.

    *   activities, resources, technology and instructional materials are all aligned to instructional purposes.

Descriptors from Texas Teacher Evaluation and Support System (T-TESS) Related to Curriculum Planning and Instruction

From The T-TESS Scoring Guide

1.1 Instructional Planning: Standards and Alignment

The teacher designs clear, well-organized, sequential lessons that reflect best practice, align with standards and are appropriate for diverse learners.

*   All goals aligned to state content standards.
*   All activities, materials and assessments that:
    *   are relevant to students
    *   provide appropriate time for lesson and lesson closure fit into the broader unit and course objectives.
    *   are appropriate for diverse learners.
*   All objectives aligned to the lesson's goal.
*   Integration of technology when applicable.

1.2 Instructional Planning: Data and Assessment

The teacher uses formal and informal methods to measure student progress, then manages and analyzes student data to inform instruction.

*   Formal and informal assessments to monitor progress of all students.

- Consistent feedback to students, families and other school personnel while maintaining confidentiality.

- Analysis of student data connected to specific instructional strategies.

1.3 Planning: Knowledge of Students

Through knowledge of students and proven practices, the teacher ensures high levels of learning, social-emotional development and achievement for all students.

- All lessons that connect to students' prior knowledge and experiences.

- Adjustments to address strengths and gaps in background knowledge, life experiences and skills of all students.

1.4 Planning: Activities

The teacher plans engaging, flexible lessons that encourage higher-order thinking, persistence and achievement.

- Questions that encourage all students to engage in complex, higher-order thinking.

- Instructional groups based on the needs of all students.

- All students understand their individual roles within instructional groups.

- Activities, resources, technology and instructional materials that are all aligned to instructional purposes.

Works Referenced

Frederick D. A. & W.C. & Klausmeier, H.G. (1969). *A scheme for testing the level of concept mastery (technical report #16)*. Madison: University of Wisconsin Research and Development Center for Cognitive Learning.

Texas Education Agency (2016). *Texas teacher evaluation and support system: T-TESS appraiser handbook*. Austin, TX.

CHAPTER 5

PLANNING THE INSTRUCTION GETTING STUDENT ATTENTION AND STUDENTS GETTING THE STUFF

The Art and Science of Teaching

Teaching is both an art and a science. The "science" of teaching is generally based on research that suggests which teaching/learning strategies produce the best student learning. These are sometime referred to as "best practices" or "research-based strategies." For many years what constitutes best practices came from psychology. Like all social sciences, psychological research did not deal in cause-effect conclusions. There are simply too many variables (student background, the quality of the teaching, available resources, fidelity to the practice, etc.) to establish cause-effect relationships. Social science research depends, instead, on correlational conclusions. Correlational research concludes that if the teacher does X, there is a high (or low) probability that the student will do Y. For example, if the teacher provides wait time between asking a question and calling on students, more students tend to engage with the question and think about a response. Statistically, there is a high statistical correlation between providing wait time and student engagement. Robert Marzano's work attempted, with great success, to synthesize this research and group the instructional practices into nine categories of instructional strategies that affect student achievement. Note that he says <u>affect</u>, not <u>cause</u>. That is really all that psychological research can do. This correlational approach has been as close to the "science" of teaching that research has been able to achieve.

Interestingly, advances in neuroscience (brain research) are just beginning to explain why and how the brain works. By using advanced technology to observe the brain, understanding how/why learning happens can move from correlational/relationship conclusions to biological conclusions. By observing what happens in the brain, we can know that if the teacher does X, the student will do Y—cause and effect.

Whether the science is based on psychological correlation or cause-effect brain research, there is a universe of tools for teachers to choose from. Which tools you ultimately choose to use is the art of teaching. Common sense and research suggest that the more students are actively involved in the learning, the better outcome you are likely to have (science). There is a huge tool kit to promote active student participation. Which ones you select to use are up to you—that's the "art" of teaching.

One caution. The strategies (art) that you select should not be based on what you like to use. Rather, when choosing strategies, they should be based on the unique needs and characteristics of the students:

- Background experiences and prior learning (their schema)
- Their interests
- Language proficiency (both oral and written)
- Reading level
- Race/ethnicity/gender
- Socio-economic background
- Presence/absence of support at home
- Learning styles

After all, it's not about you. It's about your students.

Richard James is an experienced, veteran teacher and one of my go-to experts on all things dealing with curriculum and instruction. In the process of editing this manuscript, he offered several thoughtful observations on errors he made in planning instruction.

Reflections on Planning from a Successful Veteran Teacher
Richard James, Ed.D.

I remember clearly making mistakes in planning early on in my career. I was just so overly concerned with making it through the class period without any major disruptions that I often didn't focus on the learning.

When planning for a class period's worth of instruction, many of us try to fill our 53 minutes (give or take) with bell-to-bell activities to keep everyone busy and avoid off task student behavior based on the idle hands and devil's playground theory. I call this "agenda" planning.

Wednesday:

I.   Post random bell ringer activity/journal topic to keep students occupied while I take roll.

II.   Take up homework from yesterday's lesson that we didn't have time to finish so it got sent home.

III. Assign power words vocabulary to look up and define before reading.

IV.   Open books to page ### and begin taking turns reading down the rows until page ### (We have to be through with chapter ## by the end of the week or we'll be behind the other classes.)

V.   Assign questions at the end of the section just read.

VI.   Any questions not finished during class is homework for tomorrow.

VII. Write down one thing you learned today on a post-it note and leave it on the wall by the door on your way out as an exit ticket because the principal wants everyone to do formative assessments.

Lather, rinse, repeat...

This sort of "agenda" planning is just a way to fill the period up with things to do and pays little attention to things students are supposed to learn. Because it is task/time oriented, what we're assessing and measuring are the students' ability to follow directions and keep up. This is behavior driven assessment, as in how well can I make you follow my agenda?

Real instructional design is based on what is to be learned and not what activities will fill the class period. When we focus on the objective and design an activity around the cognitive rigor or process in the standard, we can assess and measure how well students understand and can perform the learning objective.

Yes, we do have to organize our activities to take full advantage of instructional time. However, what is too often seen is more attention on the activity and less on the learning objective. Once we've taken the time to understand the standard and identify acceptable evidence of learning, we must plan an effective learning experience to support students in achieving that objective. And yes, your lesson plan may look like an outline or an agenda, but the thinking and purposeful planning behind it will allow you to assess and measure the learning and not just ritual compliance behavior.

One word of caution to those of you who resort to relying on social media sources for lesson ideas or pay other teachers for their ideas. They may look cute online and seem to make total sense on paper. However, I want to remind you all that there is a thing called "Pinterest Fail" for a reason. Just like those recipes and crafts don't always turn out like the picture, so too may your lessons not turn out well. Be a careful consumer and try things out slowly to avoid total lesson meltdown.

A Model for Planning Teaching and Learning

Instead of the "agenda" planning that Dr. James talked about, this chapter will offer you some other options. In Chapter 4 you learned how to plan the curriculum by carefully analyzing the curriculum objective: the performance standard (verb) and the content standard (stuff). Now it's time to plan how your students are going to learn that objective—the instruction.

There are many models for planning and lesson design. Unfortunately, these models are sometimes made more complicated than they need to be. In addition, the technical language and jargon of pedagogy sometimes interfere with really understanding how to design a lesson. While I will eventually get to the formal language, I want to offer what is, perhaps, an overly simplified version of a lesson design. I affectionately call it the Redneck Lesson Cycle. (Lest anyone take offense, as a native East Texan, many of my friends and family take great pride in being red necks!)

The Red Neck Lesson Cycle suggests that when you plan a lesson, there are four big chunks that you have to plan:

1. Get the students' attention.
2. The students get some stuff (the content standard of the curriculum statement).
3. The students verb the stuff (the performance standard of the curriculum statement).
4. The teacher assesses whether or not the students know the stuff and can verb it.

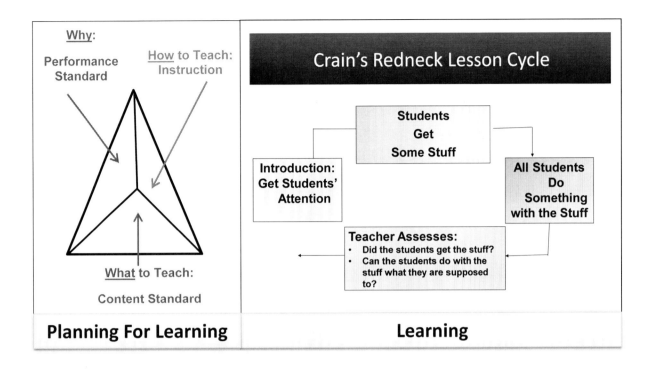

Above is a visual model of the teaching/learning cycle. The left-hand side represents planning for learning, which I discussed in Chapter 4. The right-hand side represents the teaching and learning process—four "chunks" for which you must plan.

Before analyzing and explaining how to plan each chunk, allow me to offer some caveats about interpreting and using this model. As in most models, there are limitations to this one.

Learning occurs most efficiently and effectively when the learning experience is structured.

Don't overreact to the word "structured." It does not in any way imply rigidity—it simply means that there must be some organization and structure for a lesson. How much structure is up to you. The four boxes represent what we know from the science of teaching. How and what you do to make those components happen is up to you—the virtually unlimited art of teaching.

All four components of the model do not necessarily occur in a single instructional period.

This limitation is probably the most misunderstood and abused understanding of a lesson cycle. It is not a bell-to-bell model. It is a picture of what must happen when you begin teaching a curriculum objective through the assessment of the student learning of that objective. You want to spend two days for "Students Getting Stuff?" Fine. Your decision. You want to spend three days for "All Students Doing Something with the Stuff"? Fine. Your decision. Expecting you to "get all the way through the lesson cycle" in one instructional period is not only inaccurate but, in my judgment, abusive.

There may (probably will be) more than one "box" at the top and on the right.

Each component/box typically represents one brief presentation/modeling/activity. You know that when the learning is new to students, you must organize the lesson so that you move their thinking and learning from simple to complex, concrete to abstract, and/or familiar to unfamiliar. The most common term for this thinking and learning is "scaffolding" or "chunking." The Glossary of Education Reform offers this excellent definition of scaffolding:

> In education, scaffolding refers to a variety of instructional techniques used to move students progressively toward stronger understanding and, ultimately, greater independence in the learning process. The term itself offers the relevant descriptive metaphor: teachers provide successive levels of temporary support that help students reach higher levels of comprehension and skill acquisition than they would not be able to achieve without assistance. Like physical scaffolding, the supportive strategies are incrementally removed when they are no longer needed, and the teacher gradually shifts more responsibility over the learning process to the student.
>
> Scaffolding is widely considered to be an essential element of effective teaching, and all teachers—to a greater or lesser extent—almost certainly use various forms of instructional scaffolding in their teaching. In addition, scaffolding is often used to bridge learning gaps—i.e., the difference between what students have learned and what they are expected to know and be able to do at a certain point in their education. One of the main goals of scaffolding is to reduce the negative emotions and self-perceptions that students may experience when they get frustrated, intimidated, or discouraged when attempting a difficult task without the assistance, direction, or understanding they need to complete it.

What does that have to do with the limitations of the Redneck Lesson Cycle? It means, for example, that for the top box of the cycle (Students Get Some Stuff), there may be (probably will be) more than one box. Each box represents one short presentation or activity. The science concepts of force and motion are likely abstract and unfamiliar to many students. The model has one "box" for students to learn these two concepts. You will probably need multiple "boxes" to move the student understanding from abstract/unfamiliar to concrete/familiar.

The generalization is also accurate for the other lesson components, particularly the right-hand box dealing with "Students Do Something with the Stuff." You will probably need to plan multiple activities/boxes if you want to move the "doing" from simple to complex, concrete to abstract, and/or familiar to unfamiliar.

The Redneck Lesson Cycle and Other Models of Lesson Design

Any researched-based model for teaching and learning will have the same basic components. The terminology and/or the visual model may look different, but the components are the same.

One of the earliest lesson cycles in Texas was the so-called Hunter model, based on the pioneering work of Madeline Hunter of University of California at Los Angeles. The terminology is different; the instructional components are the same.

- Focus (Anticipatory Set)
- Explanation
- Guided Practice
- Independent Practice

The "5-E Model" is another model for lesson design that has been popular in Texas. Again, the terminology is different but the components are the same:

- Engage
- Explore/Explain
- Elaborate
- Evaluate

The blue words are the Hunter Model. The red words are the 5-E model.

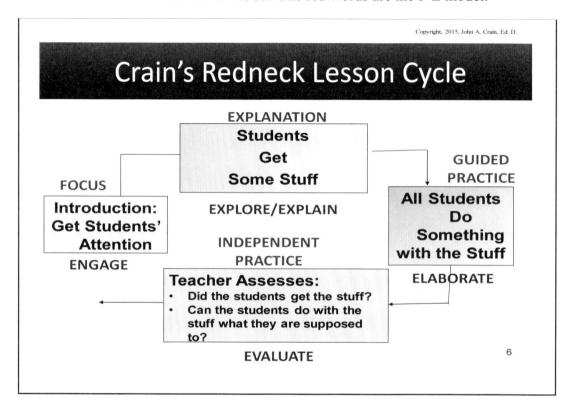

First Instructional Planning Component: Introduction—Get Student Attention

Do you assume that all of your students eagerly enter your classing crying out, "Teach me, teach me"? Right. That would be, at best, naïve. Your students enter with their own agendas: What's happening after school? Did the person I am interested in notice that I was looking at him/her? Will there be anything to eat when I get home? You must plan some way of getting your students to set aside their agendas and get on your agenda: to introduce the lesson and get them focused on the learning you have planned for them. You are attempting to tap in to what they are interested in or curious about.

This chunk of the lesson has two pieces: getting their attention and focusing them on the learning objective.

Strategies

Your art of teaching comes into play here. Here are just a few of the strategies you might consider. Which of the following fits your style and works for your students?

1. Stories/Anecdotes
    Everyone enjoys hearing an interesting story. Many successful public speakers use them to get and keep their audience engaged. It may be a personal story. It may be a

story based on a movie, television show, celebrity, or music with which your students are familiar. The story may be something that you have found in a piece of student writing or from a published source (newspaper, book, magazine). The only caveat here is that the story must have some connection to both the students' interests/curiosity and the learning objective.

2. Visuals/Graphics/Video Clips/Models/Demonstrations
    I visited a classroom in which the teacher had planned a lesson on reptiles and had placed a large glass dome over a live rattlesnake. A bit over the top perhaps, but the teacher had no further need to do anything to focus the students on the learning for the day! Somewhat less dramatic, there is a universe of images and video clips just waiting for you. Just Google UTube and you will find more interesting clips than you can possibly use.

    A variation on this strategy is to show students a picture with "speech bubbles" and ask them to fill in the bubble. Pictures of famous people and even inanimate objects can be thought provoking.

3. Rhetorical Question
    Rhetorical questions are ones that prompt an audience to think—not necessarily respond. Tell your students that you want to ask them a question to just think about—not to answer yet. Examples: How would you feel if a life-long friend suddenly abandoned you? If there were no such thing as algebra, would you still have a cell phone? What do you think would happen if the level of the Atlantic Ocean increased by three feet? If the United States decided to immediately stop using coal as a fuel, what would the next five years look like?

    If your rhetorical question evokes a "who cares" response, it's not working! The questions must tap into the students' interest and curiosity.

4. Sentence Completion
    Read an open-ended statement and ask students to think about what they would put in the blank. Examples: If I wrote a novel, it would be about___. If I could change one thing about the world we live in it would be___.

5. Find Someone Who…
    If you can tolerate some movement and noise, ask you students to find someone in the class who___. I observed an English teacher who asked his students to find someone in the class who likes poetry and why they like it. In the same vein, I observed a science teacher ask her students to find someone in the class who had a fear of spiders and why.

Second Instructional Planning Component: The Students Get Some Stuff

This is the detailed planning about how the students will get the stuff:

- Critical Attributes
- Definition
- Examples/why
- Non-examples/why

1. WHO DO YOU WANT TO DO THE WORK AND THE THINKING?

2. How much of the information (above) will you give them directly?

3. How much of the information (above) will you plan for them to discover/"figure out"?

REMEMBER: This is about students learning the CONTENT STANDARD.

1. How many different concepts did you unpack?

2. When you were unpacking the concept(s), did your work reveal other concepts that need to be either reviewed or taught?

3. When you unpacked the content standard, did you discover both a concept and a procedure?

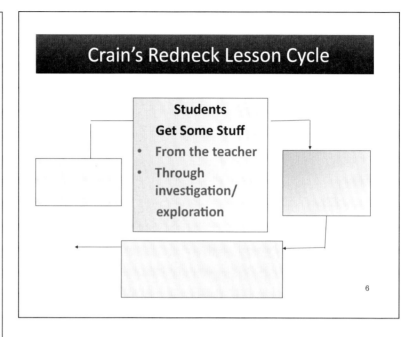

Recall from Chapter 2 that the curriculum objective has two parts: a performance standard and a content standard. The top box is all about the content standard—the stuff. This is new academic content that the students must learn. In core, cognitive curriculum, that content could be conceptual, procedural, or factual. As I have said more times than you want to read, in most cases, the content standard will be conceptual and occasionally procedural. You will need to consider how many concepts that you discovered in the content standard. In mathematics, there may be both conceptual knowledge and procedural knowledge. Let's deal with concepts first. As I explained in Chapter 4, you have already "unpacked" the content standard and you know:

- The critical attributes,

- The definition, and

- Examples and non-examples and why.

That is the stuff that the students must learn. In doing so, they will acquire a great deal of factual information about the concept, including the technical/academic language. How will they get the stuff? Well, you have two options. You can use the traditional deductive design and give them the stuff yourself, or you can plan a series of activities in which the students figure out the stuff.

You Can Give Them the Stuff

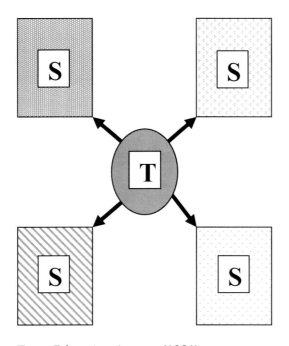

Texas Education Agency (1991)
Alternative Models of Instruction.
Austin, TX. (Visual by Ron Simpson)

Typically, you would use some variation on the lecture and question/answer format. You present the information and as frequently as possible call on students to check for understanding and probe thinking. With this model, the students tend to be passive listeners/note-takers. And why not? This model has been around forever and is the experience that most of us had in schools. Good enough for us—good enough for them.

After all, you spent at least four years in college learning this stuff, <u>you</u> are the expert, and you love hearing yourself talk about the stuff. You may have even gone back to graduate school to get some more stuff. You love your stuff!!

Now that I have, perhaps, challenged your assumptions about teaching and messed with your head a bit, I will be more serious. In a 2013 article in *The Atlantic*, Abigail Walthausen (high school English teacher), argued for the lecture approach. I present her ideas here in the interest of fairness.

Students in a lecture class can give the impression of lethargy: Maybe a student sleeps in the back of the classroom, maybe others fidget and doodle. The students who are paying attention may be too focused on their notebooks to flash a look of understanding and inspiration.

Alison King coined the flip expression "sage on the stage" in a 1997 article and, although more than half of King's article consists of ideas for working small group approaches into otherwise lecture-centric courses, demonstrating that she was in no way looking to eliminate the lecture entirely.... Nevertheless, there is immense value in lecture, and it must not be written off as boring and ineffective teaching.

Richard Gunderman argues that the "craft" of the lecture is <u>key to its value</u>, maintaining that "Good lecturing is an art, and like other arts such as painting, musicianship, and writing, it takes real dedication and many hours of practice to excel at."

Lecturing, in the sense that this article describes it, is not just standing in the front of the room and talking. As Gunderman points out, "Good lecturing is an art...." Some teachers are really good at it and are able to keep their students engaged and enthralled. They are enthusiastic, high energy, passionate, and often entertaining. Others bore you out of your socks. You have to decide whether or not the lecture/question/answer is the most effective strategy for you and for your students.

You must consider some of the advantages and disadvantages to the deductive model before making a decision.

- Advantages
  - You are a content expert. If you give the students the stuff, it will be accurate. You fear that students will not get complete and accurate information unless you control the flow of information.
  - Giving students the stuff may be a more efficient use of instructional time. You can give it to them in less time than it would take to figure it out—maybe.
  - You have a sense of greater control if everyone is quiet and have all eyes on you.
  - You are really good at it. You have passion, high energy, and the ability to keep all students highly engaged and thinking. It's fun to listen to you, the expert.

- Disadvantages
  - Students are generally passive learners and may or may not be engaged in what you are presenting.
  - Unless you have the knowledge and skill for crafting a different learning model (an inductive one), you could be wasting instructional time and allowing for behavior problems.
  - You are not an entertainer—it's just not your style or personality. While you are an expert at the content, it is difficult for you to keep all students engaged and thinking.
  - You are doing most of the work and most of the thinking.
  - A deductive, traditional lecture and question/answer structure typically begins at the Know and Understand levels and is unlikely to be any higher. While you can certainly ask higher-level questions during the presentation, only one person at a time may be thinking. Are all the other students thinking about the answer? Maybe, maybe not.

The Students Figure Out the Stuff

This is the other alternative.

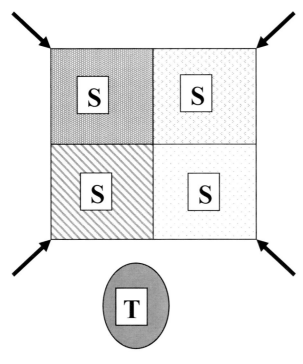

Texas Education Agency (1991)
Alternative Models of Instruction.
Austin, TX. (Visual by Ron Simpson)

Once again, you must evaluate the advantages and disadvantages of the model.

Review from Chapter 3

Review from Chapter 3

This mental model represents an inductive lesson. This lesson has a carefully designed series of tasks though which all/most of the knowledge (stuff) is obtained by the students (illustrated by the arrows NOT going from the teacher to the students). In this model, students are generally active participants in the learning. The "stuff" may come from their schema (prior experience/learning), from research, from investigation/experimentation, from each other, etc. For this process to be successful, the teacher's work is done before arriving in the classroom. There must be sufficient structure, resources, and parameters within which the student will successfully acquire the knowledge (stuff) that, in the deductive model, would have come from the teacher.

The teacher's role is to monitor and interact with students, challenge and extend their thinking, and correct and redirect when they are having difficulty.

- Advantages
  - Students are generally active learners and tend to be more engaged in what you want them to learn.
  - There is a relationship between active student engagement and motivation.
  - If you are not an entertaining, stimulating lecturer, this model increases the possibility for you to keep all students engaged and thinking.
  - The students are doing the work and the thinking.
  - Once you and your students are comfortable with the model, it can consume no more instructional time than the deductive, teacher-centered model.
  - This model typically begins at the Analyze level because students are having to discover critical attributes, organize them, and discover example/non-examples and explain why. Thus, the "top row" engages all students at a higher level of thinking from the very beginning.

- Disadvantages
  - Unless you have the knowledge and skill for crafting and structuring an inductive lesson, there is the potential for wasted instructional time and student behavior problems.
  - You may feel a loss of control, especially if you aren't comfortable with the structure of and accountability for learning.
  - Inductive learning may be appropriate for teaching conceptual and factual knowledge, but it not an efficient way to teach procedural knowledge.
  - Inductive learning may be appropriate for teaching cognitive and affective learning, but it is rarely appropriate for psychomotor learning. I doubt that you would want students to use an inductive model for learning to weld or to use a balance beam!

Scaffolding

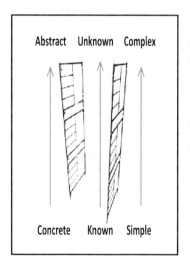

It may be that you don't have to choose one or the other. The students may get the stuff with a hybrid of the two. More about that option later.

Regardless of which model you choose, you will want to consider how much scaffolding will be needed for students to get the stuff:

- The critical attributes of the concept,
- The definition of the concept, and
- Examples and non-examples of the concept and why,
- Something fun, interesting or weird about the concept (why limit your students' learning?).

Recall that one of the limitations of the model is that "Students Get Stuff" is represented by one box on the top row. In fact, most lessons, especially concept lessons, will require some scaffolding that will be represented by more than one box on the top row. "Chunking" is another term that is sometime used as synonym for scaffolding. New learning for students may be very unfamiliar, abstract, or complex. This can be an initial turn-off for students, especially if they perceive that the learning is "too hard."

So, you must think about how many boxes you will need on the top row in order to scaffold the learning.

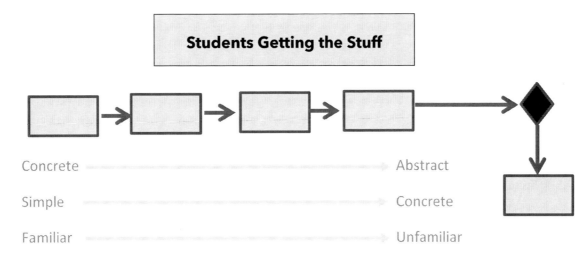

A popular scaffolded approach to teaching reading involves:

- Model Reading
- Shared Reading
- Guided Reading
- Independent Reading
- Word Work
- Writing Connections

In teaching mathematics concepts, best practices have long included using models, manipulatives, pictures, etc. at the beginning of instruction (concrete) before teaching the algorithm.

Here's a greatly oversimplified example of how the top row could be scaffolded.

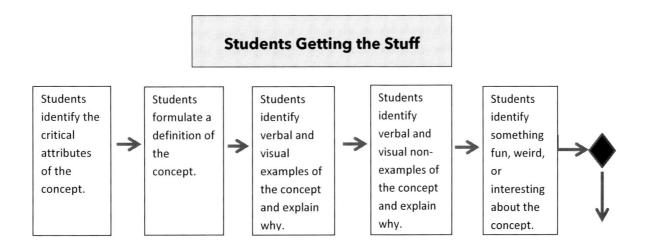

Protocol For Planning the Top Box

IF YOU WANT THE STUDENTS TO DO THE WORK AND THE THINKING ON THE TOP ROW (getting the stuff)....

1. What size groups work best for you and your students?

2. What product will students produce at the conclusion of each top row activity/box?

3. Will students have any choices about (a) how they will get the stuff and/or (b) what product they will produce at the end of each activity/box? What advantage do you see in giving the students choices?

4. How much time will you allocate for each top row activity/box?

As you plan each of the scaffolded boxes, the following is the set of decisions that you must make while planning.

Groups: What size and what criteria will you use for the grouping? How will you assign any roles/responsibilities?

Student Product(s) at the end of each top row activity/ box:

a. Will you provide advanced organizers/thinking maps/partial outlines, etc.

b. What will students have produced (oral and/or written) that shows that they have the definition, critical attributes, and examples/non-examples of the concept(s)?

Student Choice:

a. What choices, if any, will students have about how they will discover the stuff?

b. What choices, if any, will students have about the product they produce and how they will produce it?

Resources:

a. What resources will the students need to get "the stuff" (definition, critical attributes, examples, non-examples)?

b. How can technology assist this task?

c. Will you need to provide materials?

Time Limits

How much time will you allocate for each activity/box?

Planning for this model is very different. You can't just say to students "get into groups and…" Disaster!

When the Knowledge is Procedural or Factual

Remember that procedural knowledge consists of students learning the critical attributes of the procedure: steps and/or rules. Remember, also, that most procedures are based on one or more concepts. Without understanding the concept(s) on which the procedure is based, students may have little understanding of what they are doing and why. I recommend that you consider an inductive model for students to learn the concept. Then design a teacher-centered, deductive model for students to learn the steps/rules. If they have a deep understanding of the concept(s), learning the steps/rules will be easier. For example, if you are teaching the concepts of *area* and *perimeter*, use an inductive model for the top row followed by a teacher-centered, deductive model for the formulas. Without understanding the concept(s) on which the procedure is based, students may have little understanding of what they are doing and why.

WITHOUT UNDERSTANDING THE CONCEPT(S) ON WHICH THE PROCEDURE IS BASED, STUDENTS MAY HAVE LITTLE UNDERSTANDING OF WHAT THEY ARE DOING AND WHY.

Factual knowledge is the most boring for students to engage in unless you are one of those exceptional entertainers. The information is in a book, a video clip, on a handout, or on-line. So design an inductive model for them to get the facts, following the protocol previously discussed in this chapter.

A Note on Differentiation

With shifting student demographics across school districts, differentiation of instruction has never been more important. This chapter addresses initial instructional design and will not deal in any depth with differentiation. In a series of wonderful books, Carol Ann Tomlinson (whom I consider the guru of differentiation) has written extensively on this subject. You will find her publications cited at the end of the chapter.

She basically proposes that you can differentiate three major elements of the instruction:

- The content (different content for different students)
- The process (different processes by which students will learn the content)
- The performance (different ways that students can demonstrate that they have learned)

With state and district curriculum standards, it is difficult to differentiate the content. It is prescribed in the content standard of the curriculum.

The greatest opportunities for differentiation lie in the process of learning the stuff and performance (what they will do with the stuff). To correlate with the Redneck Lesson Cycle language, you can differentiate the top row—how the students will get the content/stuff (the process). You can also differentiate the side row—what students will do with the content/stuff (the performance).

Structure the lesson so that your students are in charge of the learning, doing most of the work, doing most of the thinking, and making more choices—an inductive model. Allow them to be in charge of finding the stuff and doing something with it. If you do that, many students will provide their own differentiation. No student says, "I have to learn this, so I will find the most difficult way possible for me to learn it." If you allow them the opportunity, they will find the best way for <u>them</u> to learn and demonstrate to you that they have learned.

You may also want to examine the language of the Texas Teacher Assessment and Support System (T-TESS) dealing with this issue: *Instruction 2.4: Differentiation*: The teacher differentiates instruction, aligning methods and techniques to diverse student needs. Those descriptors are at the end of this chapter.

SUMMARY

1. Teaching is both an art and a science. The science of teaching is based on psychological research and relationships and/or neuroscience research and cause/effect relationships. Whether they are called "best practices" or "research-based strategies," it's the science of teaching. The art of teaching is yours. From an immense toolbox of methods and strategies based on the science, which ones work best for you and your students?

2. The first instructional component you have to plan is something to get them to engage with you and the learning.

3. The second instructional component is the "top row"—students get some stuff. This component is all about the content standards (stuff).

4. You have two options for designing how students will get the stuff: a teacher-centered, deductive model or a student-centered inductive model. No matter which model you choose, there will be advantages and disadvantages.

5. Regardless of which model you choose, you will need to consider some scaffolding (chunking) of the learning.

As you plan the lesson and think about making certain that your students are initially engaged and "get the stuff" (the content standard), ask yourself these questions:

1. What will I do to engage all my students with me and with the learning?

2. What activities will I use so that my students "get the stuff" (content standard)—a teacher-centered, deductive model or a student-centered inductive model? What advantages and disadvantages of each approach am I considering?

3. How can I scaffold (chunk) the top row ("students are getting the stuff") so my students are not overwhelmed with too much stuff all at one time?

4. What activities can I plan so that all students:

   • Respond to questions and tasks at all levels of Bloom's Taxonomy of Cognitive Learning?

   • Discuss the learning and respond to your probing questions to clarify and elaborate the learning?

5. How can I maximize opportunities for all my students to communicate effectively with me and with their peers?

6. What can I do to adapt the lessons to address individual needs of all my students?

7. What am I planning so that I can monitor the quality of student participation and performance as they engage in the learning?

8. If my students become confused or disengaged, what do I have in my tool kit that I can use to respond to their learning and/or social/emotional needs?

Most teacher evaluation systems express expectations about your use of the design of the instruction—the actual lesson. Obviously, you want to know and follow your district's expectations.

Descriptors from Texas Teacher Evaluation and Support System (T-TESS) Related to Getting Student Attention and Students Getting the Stuff

From the T-TESS Scoring Guide

Instruction 2.1 Achieving Expectations

The teacher supports all learners in their pursuit of high levels of academic and social-emotional success.

- Sets academic expectations that challenge all students.

- Persists with the lesson until there is evidence that most students demonstrate mastery of the objective.

- Addresses student mistakes and follows through to ensure student mastery.

- Provides students opportunities to take initiative of their own learning.

Instruction 2.2 Content Knowledge and Expertise

The teacher uses content and pedagogical expertise to design and execute lessons aligned with state standards, related content and student needs.

- Conveys accurate content knowledge in multiple contexts.

- Integrates learning objectives with other disciplines.

- Anticipates possible student misunderstandings.

- Provides opportunities for students to use different types of thinking (e.g., analytical, practical, creative and research-based).

- Accurately reflects how the lesson fits within the structure of the discipline and the state standards.

Instruction 2.3 Communication

The teacher clearly and accurately communicates to support persistence, deeper learning and effective effort.

- Establishes classroom practices that provide opportunities for most students to communicate effectively with the teacher and their peers.

- Recognizes student misunderstandings and responds with an array of teaching techniques to clarify concepts.

- Provides explanations that are clear and uses verbal and written communication that is clear and correct.

- Asks remember, understand and apply level questions that focus on the objective of the lesson and provoke discussion.

- Uses probing questions to clarify and elaborate learning.

Instruction 2.4: Differentiation

The teacher differentiates instruction, aligning methods and techniques to diverse student needs.

- Adapts lessons to address individual needs of all students.

- Regularly monitors the quality of student participation and performance.

- Provides differentiated instructional methods and content to ensure students have the opportunity to master what is being taught.

- Recognizes when students become confused or disengaged and responds to student learning or social/emotional needs.

Instruction 2.5: Monitor and Adjust

- Consistently invites input from students in order to monitor and adjust instruction and activities.

- Adjusts instruction and activities to maintain student engagement.

- Monitors student behavior and responses for engagement and understanding.

Works Referenced

Anderson, L. W., Krathwohl, D.R., et. al. (2010). *A taxonomy for learning, teaching, and assessing: A revision of Bloom's taxonomy of educational objectives.* New York: Longman.

Bloom, B. S., Ebglehart, Max D., et al. (1956). *The taxonomy of educational objectives, the classification of educational goals, handbook I: cognitive domain.* New York: David McKay Company, Inc.

Hunter, Madeline (1982). *Mastery teaching.* El Segundo, CA. TIPS Publications.

Marzano, Robert, Pickering, Debra J, and Pollock, James E. (2001). *Classroom instruction that works: research-based strategies for increasing student achievement.* Alexandria, VA: Association for Supervision and Curriculum Development.

Texas Education Agency (2001), *Alternative models of instruction*, Austin, Texas.

Texas Education Agency (2016). *Texas teacher evaluation and support system: T-TESS appraiser handbook.* Austin, TX.

Tomlinson, Carol Ann. (2017, 3rd Edition.). *How to differentiate instruction in academically diverse classrooms.* New York: Association for Supervision and Curriculum Development.

Other representative work by Carol Ann Tomlinson and published by Association for Supervision and Curriculum Development:

- *Assessment and student success in a differentiated classroom* (2015).
- *Leading and managing a differentiated classroom* (2010).

Walthauson, Abigail. (November 21, 2013). "Don't give up on the lecture." The Atlantic. Retrieved from https://www.theatlantic.com/education/archive/2013/11/dont-give-up-on-the-lecture/281624/

CHAPTER 6

STUDENTS DO SOMETHING WITH THE STUFF (ELABORATION; GUIDED PRACTICE)

Now that students have the content standard (stuff), what will they do with it?

IF YOU WANT STUDENTS TO HAVE A DEEP UNDERSTANDING OF THE CONTENT AND YOU WANT THEM TO HAVE ANY CHANCE AT LONG-TERM RETENTION, THEY MUST DO SOMETHING WITH THE STUFF.

Why Is This A Critical Issue?

Whether you chose a deductive model or inductive model for the top row (students get the stuff), you must now plan for the right side—All Students Do Something With the Stuff.

In all too many lessons, the students get stuff (top box of the Redneck Lesson Cycle) and are then required to regurgitate the stuff on some kind of paper/pencil assessment (on the bottom row). If all you want them to get is content knowledge, then the box on the right side would be unnecessary. Some teachers argue that there is so much curriculum to cover that there simply isn't enough time to devote to student activities where they work together to process and apply the information. However, if you want students to have a deep understanding of the content and you want them to have any chance at long-term retention, they must do something with the stuff. If they do not, they get, at best, short-term retention. Retention and transfer of learning will be explained more fully in Chapter 9. In order for new knowledge to go into long-term memory, the brain needs to process the information (Apply, Analyze, Evaluate, Create). Chapter 3 introduced you to the idea of the performance standards—the verb in its context. This is the point in your planning at which you begin to envision what <u>all</u> students will be doing with the stuff. What will it look like and sound like? How will it be structured?

As indicated on the model below, the students must do at least two things with the stuff:

1. They must verb the stuff.

2. They must connect the stuff to process skills.

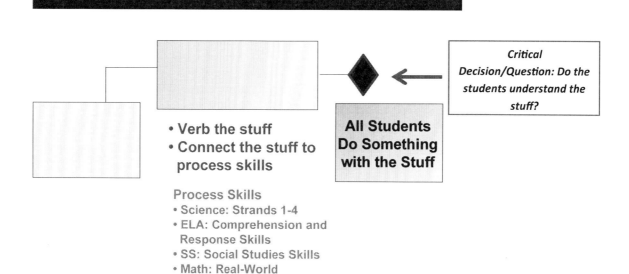

Verbing the Stuff

The performance standard of the curriculum has a verb—at a minimum, that's what students should be doing with the stuff. From the examples in Chapter 2, look at the following performance standards. If I were to observe in your classroom on a day on which you and your students were on the right-hand side, this is what I might see them all doing.

model the relationship between	describe and explain the effects	demonstrate
use concrete models to demonstrate	calculate unit rates	create
analyze and evaluate the relationship	use a problem-solving model	invent images
describe the interactions among	express and manipulate chemical quantities	

For this to happen, you would need to design an activity (more likely a series of activities) for students to exhibit these behaviors.

Connecting the Stuff to "Process Skills"

In most curriculum standards, there is a set of curriculum objectives that is process skills; there is no academic content connected to these skills—they are thinking processes that students should be able to demonstrate with any academic content. There is sometimes the sense of "oh, we do that all the time." If that's the assumption, it is unlikely that most of your students will retain much of what you wanted them to learn. Integrating the process skills cannot be effectively learned through such a serendipitous approach. You must plan the right hand box to intentionally cause the thinking process to occur. I call that "marrying the process skills to the content standard (stuff)."

In social studies, curriculum standards consist of multiple sets of processes. Consider these examples from 8th grade United States History:

Social studies skills. The student applies critical-thinking skills to organize and use information acquired through established research methodologies from a variety of valid sources, including electronic technology. The student is expected to: *There are ten different skills listed, A-J.)*

Social studies skills. The student communicates in written, oral, and visual forms. The student is expected to: *(There are four different processes skills listed, A-D.)*

In science, the first strands of curriculum objectives are multiple sets of scientific processes and thinking. Consider the examples from high school biology:

Scientific processes. The student uses scientific methods and equipment during laboratory and field investigations. The student is expected to: *(There are eight different process skills listed, A-H.)*

Scientific processes. The student uses critical thinking, scientific reasoning, and problem solving to make informed decisions within and outside the classroom. The student is expected to: *(There are six different process skills listed.)*

In mathematics, the first strands of curricuum objectives are sets of mathematical thinking and reasoning. Consider the example from 5th grade mathematics:

Mathematical process standards. The student uses mathematical processes to acquire and demonstrate mathematical understanding. The student is expected to: *(There are seven different process skills listed, A-G)*

Finally, in English Language Arts/Reading, the process skills are found in the Comprehension Skills and the Response Skills (formerly Figure 19). Consider the example from 6th grade ELA/R:

Comprehension Skills: make inferences and use evidence to support understanding.

There is a state assessment (STAAR) issue involved here. You are familiar with the concept of "dual coding" of assessment items. That means that the test item assesses two different curriculum standards <u>at the same time.</u> Generally, one of the curiculum standards asseses verbing the stuff: *use strategies and algorithms, including the standard algorithm, to multiply a two-digit number by a one-digit number.* Sounds pretty simple, doesn't it—multiply a two-digit number by a one-digit number. Think about what happens if the assessment asks students to connect that content to one of the process skills: *use a problem-solving model that incorporates analyzing given information, formulating a plan or strategy, determining a solution, justifying the solution and evaluating the problem-solving process and the reasonableness of the solution.*

On one recent STAAR test, a problem that was dual coded to these curriculum standards was one of the most frequently missed in the state. The assessment item did not simply give students a problem where they had to multiple a two-digit number by a one-digit. To solve the problem, students had to first know that multiplication was the mathematical operation they needed to use. Then they had to multiply two times; <u>then</u> they had to add the two products (answers) together to get the correct answer.

What makes STAAR more difficult/rigorous than its predecessors? It's the dual coding. So, if you are not regularly and intentionally imbedding the process skills into your lessons, your students are in big trouble when it's time for the state assessment.

OK. So now you know that there are at least two things that all the students should be doing with the stuff on the right-hand side of the cycle: verbing it and connecting it to one or more of the process skills. How can that connecting work?

When you know that the students understand the stuff (critical attributes, definition, examples/why, non-examples/why), they are ready to turn the corner to the right-hand side.

Non-Negotiable: All students most practice and demonstrate that they can:

1. Verb the stuff and

2. Marry/connect one or more of the process skills to the content standard (stuff).

---

1. What product will students produce at the conclusion of each right-hand side activity/box?

2. How will students work together to produce these products?

3. Will students have any choices about (a) how they can verb the stuff and marry/connect process skills to the stuff and/or (b) what product they will produce at the end of each activity/box? What advantage do you see in giving the students choices?

4. What resources will students need? How can technology add interest or quality?

5. How will you scaffold the right side?

6. How much time will you allocate for each right-hand side activity/box?

Protocol for Planning

1. Student Product(s) at the end of each right-hand activity/box:

   a. What will students have produced (oral and/or written) that shows that they can:

   > i. Verb the stuff?

   > ii. Marry one or more of the process to the concept(s)?

   b. How can students use technology to produce the product(s)?

2. How will you organize students to <u>work together</u>?

3. Student Choice: Will students have any choices about

   a. How they will demonstrate that they can verb the stuff and marry/connect process skills to the stuff?

   b. What product(s) they will produce at the end of each activity/box?

4. Resources: What resources will the students need, if any? How will technology add interest or quality?

5. Scaffolding: How might you scaffold the right side for stronger learning? Will the side row be one activity or a series of scaffolded activities (from simple to more complex; from concrete to more abstract; from familiar to more unfamiliar)?

6. Time Limits: How much time will you allocate for each right-hand side activity/box?

The following is a rather simple example of what verbing the stuff and marrying/connecting process skills might look like. Your primary curriculum objective was: *Students are expected to determine the figurative meaning of phrases and analyze how an author's use of language creates imagery, appeals to the senses, and suggests mood.* You chose another curriculum objective from the process skills: *Students are expected to make complex inferences about text and use textual evidence to support understanding.*

On the top row/box, students learned about "figurative meaning of phrases" and their impact on the reader or listener. You told them (or you allowed them figured out) the critical attributes of figurative language, working definitions, and examples/non-examples and why. They also learned that the use of figurative phrases creates mental images, causes a sensory reaction, and causes various emotional responses from the reader. Good information. Now, what will they do with it?

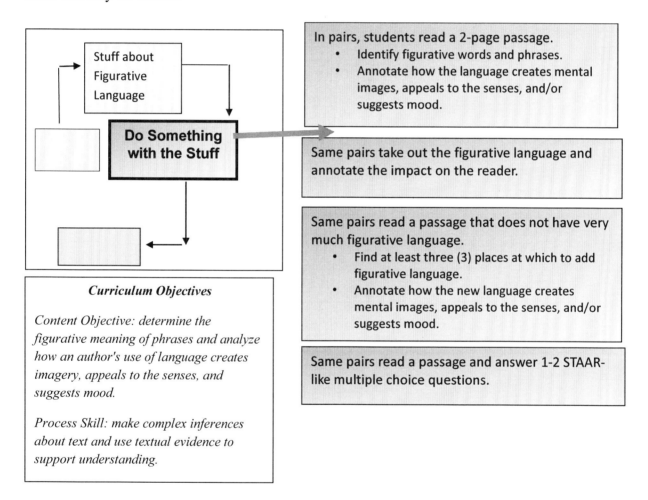

Curriculum Objectives

Content Objective: determine the figurative meaning of phrases and analyze how an author's use of language creates imagery, appeals to the senses, and suggests mood.

Process Skill: make complex inferences about text and use textual evidence to support understanding.

Looking back at the six questions that you asked in planning this part of the lesson, there are several things that you should notice:

- <u>All</u> students are verbing the stuff—*determining the figurative meaning of phrases and analyzing how an author's use of language creates imagery, appeals to the senses, and suggests mood.*

- <u>All</u> students are also marrying/connecting one of the process skills to the content— *making complex inferences about text (in this case about the figurative meaning of phrases and its impact on the reader and use textual evidence to support understanding.* The lesson is scaffolded; one activity leads into the other.

- Students are working together. They are still learning. They learn together; they will be assessed individually on the bottom of the Redneck Lesson Cycle. **You cannot cheat <u>while you are learning</u>.**

- They are producing a product at each stage of the learning.

- With some sadness, I have included the fourth activity dealing with state assessment. I might or might not actually ask students to do that, depending on the time of year or the needs of the students in the group.

The following is a second example (from social studies) of what "Students Doing Something With the Stuff" might look like. This one is a little more complex because of the number of concepts in the curriculum statement and because of the process skill that is included.

Your primary curriculum objective is: *identify the characteristics of the following political systems: theocracy, absolute monarchy, democracy, republic, oligarchy, limited monarchy, and totalitarianism.*

You chose another curriculum objective from the social studies process skills: *The student is expected to analyze information by categorizing, ~~identifying cause-and-effect relationships,~~ comparing, contrasting, ~~finding the main idea, summarizing, making generalizations and predictions~~, drawing inferences and conclusions, and developing connections between historical events over time.* Note that some of the process skills are struck through. That is because you are intentionally planning for only some of them in the activities you are planning. It does not mean that the other thinking will not take place; it simply means that you are intentionally planning for the others to happen.

On the top row, students learned about "political systems." That's the primary concept. The other things in the list are examples of political systems. Don't get confused and conclude that the primary learning is about theocracy, absolute monarchy, etc. This is one of those lessons in which students will not have to discover examples. The examples of "political systems" are already in the curriculum objective. You still will probably want them to figure out some <u>non-examples and why</u>. On the top row, you told them (or you have allowed them to figure out) the critical attributes of <u>any</u> political system, a working definition, examples and non-examples and why. Good information. Now, what will they do with it? Again, there are more scaffolded activities in this example because of the multiple examples of political systems in the curriculum objective and the variety of thinking you want your students to do.

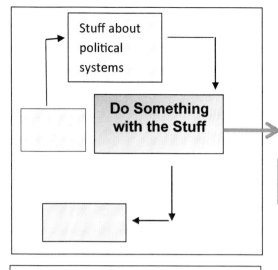

In pairs, students do research (print/electronic) to identify one historical example of any <u>two</u> of the political systems.

Same pairs compare and contrast <u>two</u> of the political systems based on the critical attributes of a political system.

In pairs, students identify advantages and disadvantages of each political system.

Combine groups. In groups <u>of four</u>, create a comparison/contrast chart/diagram using the two political systems from each pair.

Same groups of four do research (print/electronic) to identify a <u>contemporary example</u> each of their four political systems.

Same groups of four rank-order their four political systems based on the systems' effectiveness and make a case for their rankings.

Same groups report out their findings using available technology.

Same groups answer 1-2 "STAAR-like" multiple choice questions.

Curriculum Objectives

Identify the characteristics of the following political systems: theocracy, absolute monarchy, democracy, republic, oligarchy, limited monarchy, and totalitarianism.

Analyze information by categorizing, comparing, contrasting, drawing inferences and conclusions, and developing connections between historical events over time.

Scaffolded Planning

Wow! That looks like a lot, and it is. But remember that the curriculum objective has seven examples of political systems that you must deal with.

[Political and editorial comment: Even though <u>communism</u> is not in the list, I would probably add it. After all, China, Vietnam, and Cuba still retain some version of that political system. How does one understand The Cold War and the Vietnam War without understanding this political system?! It was perhaps left out of the state's curriculum standards because someone feared you might teach your students to be communists.]

Looking back at the six questions that you asked in planning this part of the lesson, there are several things that you should notice:

- <u>All</u> students are verbing the stuff—*identifying the characteristics of the following political systems: theocracy, absolute monarchy, democracy, republic, oligarchy, limited monarchy, and totalitarianism.*

- <u>All</u> students are also marrying/connecting one of the process skills to the content—*analyzing information by categorizing, comparing, contrasting, drawing inferences and conclusions, and developing connections between historical events over time.*

- The lesson is scaffolded; one activity leads into the other.

- Students are working together. They are still learning. They learn together; they will be assessed individually on the bottom of the cycle.

- They are producing a product at each stage of the learning.

- Again, with some sadness, I have included the last activity dealing with state assessment. I might or might not actually ask students to do that.

A Note on Project-Based Learning

I would argue both examples above represent project-based learning (depending on whose definition you use). One of the differences between this model and other versions of project-based learning is that you did not begin with (front-load) a project and then have the students learn whatever they need to learn in order to produce the product (backload). You began, as you should have, with the curriculum standards—you front-loaded the curriculum. Based on both the content standard and the performance standard, you designed a series of activities in which students produced one or more products (backload).

A Note on Differentiation

I refer you again to the insights of Carol Ann Tomlinson. You will find her publications cited at the end of the chapter.

Remember that she proposes that you can differentiate three major elements of the instruction:

- The content (different content for different students)

- The process (different processes by which students will learn the content)

- The performance (different ways that students can demonstrate that they have learned)

Since this chapter deals with "Students Doing Something with the Stuff," this is what Tomlinson refers to as the performance.

Structure the lesson so that

- your students are in charge of the learning;
- they are doing most of the work;
- they doing most of the thinking; and
- they are making more choices.

Allow them to be in charge of doing something with the learning. If you do that, many students will provide their own differentiation. Many students will seek out their own differentiation. Again, no student says, "I have to learn this, so I will find the most difficult way possible for me to learn it." If you allow them the opportunity, they will find the best way for them to learn and demonstrate to you that they have learned.

"Taking Grades"

<Sigh> Remember: the students are still learning on the right-hand side of the Redneck Lesson Cycle. When your students are "Doing Something with the Stuff," they are practicing. Occasionally, they are practicing some kind of procedural knowledge: mathematical algorithms or language mechanics (spelling, grammar, punctuation). Most often they should be practicing thinking about the content standard (the stuff).

Yes, you are assessing whatever you are having your students do here. This is formative assessment, NOT summative. You are simply monitoring their progress, giving them feedback, and adjusting when necessary. More on formative and summative assessment in the next chapter.

Why in the world would you want to "take a grade" while they are still learning?! A German student told me one time, "American schools are unfair." Somewhat defensively, I asked him, "Why?" His response: "You grade me before I have learned. You should not grade me until after I have learned." Food for thought.

Summary

- The right-side box of the cycle addresses students doing something with the content standard (stuff).
- If they do not practice thinking and processing the content standard (stuff), the outcome is likely to be superficial understanding and short-term retention.
- Students are working together to produce products. Their products will tell you if they:

- understand the content/stuff,
- can at least verb the stuff, and
- marry/connect the process skills to the content/stuff.

- The learning was scaffolded. By the end, the students got where you wanted them to be. You just did it in little bites.

Most teacher evaluation systems express expectation about your use of the design of the instruction—the actual lesson. Obviously, you want to know and follow your district's expectations. As you plan the lesson and begin to think about students "doing something with the stuff," ask yourself these questions:

1. How can I scaffold (chunk) the side row/box ("students doing somethings with the stuff") so my students are not overwhelmed with too many complex tasks all at one time?

2. What activities can I plan so that all students are:
   - "Verbing the Stuff"?
   - Marrying/connecting higher-level thinking processes to the stuff?

3. How can I maximize opportunities for all my students to communicate effectively with me and with their peers as they are verbing the stuff?

4. What product(s) will my students produce to show that they can successfully verb the stuff and marry higher-level thinking process to the stuff?

5. What can I do to adapt the right side/box of the lesson cycle to address individual needs of all my students?

6. What am I planning so that I can monitor the quality of student participation and performance as they engage in verbing the stuff?

7. If my students become confused or disengaged, what do I have in my tool kit that I can use to respond to their learning and/or social/emotional needs?

Descriptors from Texas Teacher Evaluation and Support System (T-TESS) Related to Verbing the Stuff and Integrating Process Skills

From the T-TESS Scoring Guide

Instruction 2.1 Achieving Expectations

The teacher supports all learners in their pursuit of high levels of academic and social-emotional success.

- Sets academic expectations that challenge all students.

- Persists with the lesson until there is evidence that most students demonstrate mastery of the objective.

- Addresses student mistakes and follows through to ensure student mastery.

- Provides students opportunities to take initiative of their own learning.

Instruction 2.2 Content Knowledge and Expertise

The teacher uses content and pedagogical expertise to design and execute lessons aligned with state standards, related content and student needs.

- Conveys accurate content knowledge in multiple contexts.

- Integrates learning objectives with other disciplines.

- Anticipates possible student misunderstandings.

- Provides opportunities for students to use different types of thinking (e.g., analytical, practical, creative and research-based).

- Accurately reflects how the lesson fits within the structure of the discipline and the state standards.

Instruction 2.3 Communication

The teacher clearly and accurately communicates to support persistence, deeper learning and effective effort.

- Establishes classroom practices that provide opportunities for most students to communicate effectively with the teacher and their peers.

- Recognizes student misunderstandings and responds with an array of teaching techniques to clarify concepts.

- Provides explanations that are clear and uses verbal and written communication that is clear and correct.

- Asks remember, understand and apply level questions that focus on the objective of the lesson and provoke discussion.

- Uses probing questions to clarify and elaborate learning.

Instruction 2.4: Differentiation

The teacher differentiates instruction, aligning methods and techniques to diverse student needs.

- Adapts lessons to address individual needs of all students.

- Regularly monitors the quality of student participation and performance.

- Provides differentiated instructional methods and content to ensure students have the opportunity to master what is being taught.

- Recognizes when students become confused or disengaged and responds to student learning or social/emotional needs.

<u>Instruction 2.5: Monitor and Adjust</u>

- Consistently invites input from students in order to monitor and adjust instruction and activities.

- Adjusts instruction and activities to maintain student engagement.

- Monitors student behavior and responses for engagement and understanding.

Works Referenced

Texas Education Agency (2016). *Texas teacher evaluation and support system: T-TESS appraiser handbook.* Austin, TX.

Tomlinson, Carol Ann (2017, 3rd Edition). *How to differentiate instruction in academically diverse classrooms.* New York: Association for Supervision and Curriculum Development.

Other representative work by Carol Ann Tomlinson and published by Association for Supervision and Curriculum Development:

- *Assessment and student success in a differentiated classroom* (2015).

- *Leading and managing a differentiated classroom* (2010).

CHAPTER 7

STUDENTS DEMONSTRATE THAT THEY HAVE LEARNED (EVALUATION; INDEPENDENT PRACTICE)

This chapter focuses on the "bottom box" of the Redneck Lesson Cycle and reflects summative (versus formative) assessment.

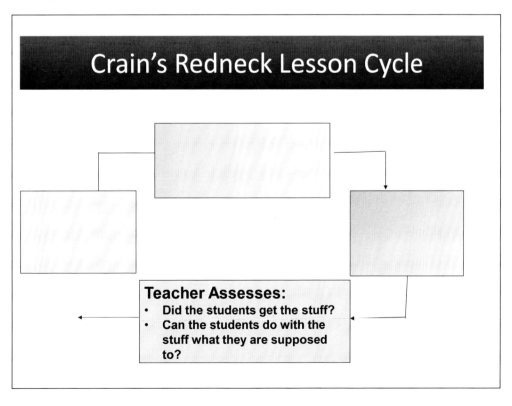

Formative and Summative Assessment

From a classroom perspective, you are generally engaged in two kinds of assessment:

- Formative Assessment: Assessing <u>for</u> learning (the top box and the right box)
- Summative Assessment: Assessment <u>of</u> learning (the bottom box)

Tom Angelo summarized assessment this way:

"Assessment is an ongoing process aimed at understanding and improving student learning. It involves making our expectations explicit and public; setting appropriate criteria and high standards for learning quality; systematically gathering, analyzing, and interpreting evidence to determine how well performance matches those expectations and standards; and using the resulting information to document, explain, and improve performance...." (Skidmore College)

Jay Mctighe and Ken O'Connor offer the following explanations of formative and summative assessment.

"*Formative Assessment* is generally carried out throughout a course or project (or lesson). Formative assessment ... is used to aid learning. In an educational setting, formative assessment might be a teacher, a peer, or the learner providing feedback on a student's work and would not necessarily be used for grading purposes. Formative assessments can take the form of diagnostic, standardized tests, quizzes, oral question, or draft work. Formative assessments are carried out concurrently with instruction. The formative assessments aim to see if the students understand the instruction before doing a summative assessment." (Mctighe and O'Conner)

In the previous chapter, I suggested that when the students are "Doing Something with the Stuff," they are <u>practicing</u>. In pairs or triads, students should be producing products, performances, and/or demonstrations in which they are "verbing the stuff" and "marrying/connecting processes skills" to the academic content (the stuff). Your role is to monitor the work, provide feedback, and make whatever adjustments are necessary. This is your best opportunity to assess their learning <u>formatively</u>.

"*Summative assessment* is generally carried out at the end of a unit, project, or course. In an educational setting, summative assessments are typically used to assign students a unit grade. Summative assessments are evaluative. Summative assessments are designed to determine what the students have learned, to determine whether they understand the subject matter well. ... A criticism of summative assessments is that they are reductive, and learners discover how well they have acquired knowledge too late for it to be of use." (Mctighe and O'Conner)

Limitations of Traditional Assessment

Traditional assessments have all too frequently been in the form of paper-pencil "tests." These include:

- True/False
- Fill-in-the-Blank
- Matching
- Short Answer
- Multiple Choice

There are a number of significant limitations to these tests.

Recalling the curriculum language from Chapter 1, these traditional assessments are assessing the content standard, <u>not the performance standard</u>. At best, they are testing short-term recall at the Know level of Bloom's Taxonomy. They tell you nothing about the students' real understanding of the content; **only having them <u>do</u> something with the content can tell you that.**

They may be assessing compliance rather than real learning. Is the student willing to memorize and regurgitate X number of spelling words, names, dates, places, academic terminology? That's not a great intellectual power. Phillip C. Schlechty was founder and CEO of the Schlechty Center for Leadership in School Reform. Schlechty was the author of Leading for *Learning, Creating Great Schools, Working on the Work, Inventing Better Schools, Shaking Up the Schoolhouse, and Schools for the 21st Century.*

I recall many years ago hearing Schlechty tell an audience that there are three rules for success in too many classrooms:

1. Take Orders.
2. Do meaningless tasks without being bothered by them and with a reasonable level of enthusiasm.
3. Tolerate boredom.

Do you have a decent grade on a transcript for a class in which you learned nothing? How did you pass/make a decent grade: probably by following Schlechty's three rules. Sadly, there are classrooms in which this is true. The grades that students receive may be more of a measure of their compliance rather than of their learning. Unfortunately, dealing with letter and number grades are still an issue that you will face. I will have more to say about this issue when I discuss products and rubrics later in this chapter.

Summative Assessment: MUST MATCH THE RIGHT SIDE

How will students individually demonstrate that they have:

1. learned the content standard—the stuff?

2. performed at the level of the performance standard—the verb and its modifiers?

3. married the concept(s) with one or more process skills?

Note: Individual work: "learn together; individually accountable."

Note: Must match the right-hand box—assess the learning in the same way it was learned/practiced in the right side; no surprises.

Protocol for Planning Summative Assessment

When students were "doing something with the stuff" in the right-hand box, they were dealing with the content standards (the stuff), verbing the stuff, and marrying/connecting process skills to the stuff. Madeline Hunter called this Guided Practice; the 5-E model called this Elaboration. Practice is a perfectly acceptable term, if you consider that they are practicing thinking about the stuff. Hopefully, all of that practice was in pairs, triads, or quads—students thinking and practicing together. All this culminates in the assessment that calls for students to independently demonstrate that they:

- Know the Stuff
- Can Verb the Stuff
- Can Marry/Connect Process Skills to the Content Standard

Matching the Right-Hand Box With the Bottom Box—Aligning the Instruction and The Assessment

In the summative assessment (bottom box), each student will complete a product, performance, or demonstration. The summative assessment must <u>match what they did when they were Doing Something with the Stuff" (right-hand side box)</u>. Why would you even consider assessing them in a way that is different from the way they practiced? The following are extensions of the examples of Students Doing Something With the Stuff (right-hand box) from the previous chapter. They illustrate the principle of matching the formative practice with the summative assessment.

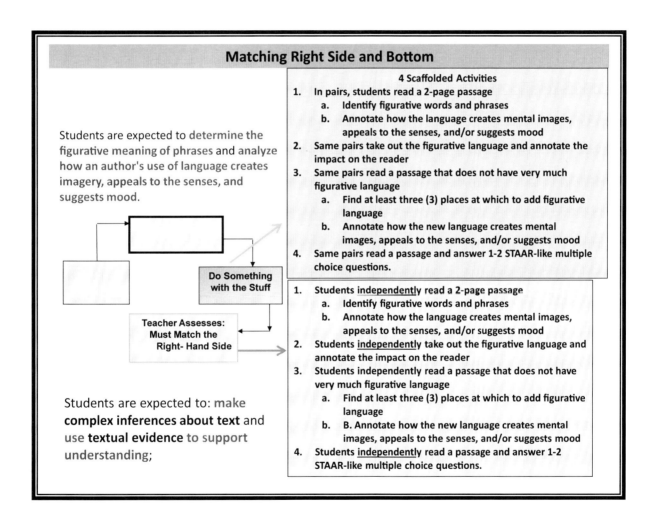

Note that the work students are doing at the bottom for summative assessment matches what they did on the right-hand side when Doing Something With the Stuff.

Assessment Rubrics

OK. Now how do you "grade" the students' final products, performance, or demonstration? You will need a rubric that specifies different qualities of the product(s). There are two primary kinds of assessment rubrics: holistic and analytical. An excellent source for more detail is Susan M. Brookhart's <u>How to Create and Use Rubrics for Formative Assessment and Grading</u>. She defines the two different rubrics in the following way:

> *Analytic rubrics* describe work on each criterion separately. *Holistic rubrics* describe the work by applying all the criteria at the same time and enabling an overall judgment about the quality of the work….
>
> For most classroom purposes, analytic rubrics are best. Focusing on the criteria one at a time is better for instruction and better for formative assessment because students can see what aspects of their work need what kind of attention. Focusing on the criteria one at a time is good for any summative assessment (grading) that will also be used to make decisions about the future—for example, decisions about how to follow up on a unit or decisions about how to teach something next year.

The State of Texas Assessment of Academic Readiness (STAAR) writing assessment is an example of a holistic rubric. There are three criteria for scoring the students writing:

- Organization/Progression

- Development of Ideas

- Use of Language/Conventions

When scoring the students' writing, the rubric describes four levels of performance:

- Score Point 1: The essay represents a very limited writing performance.

- Score Point 2: The essay represents a basic writing performance.

- Score Point 3: The essay represents a satisfactory writing performance.

- Score Point 4: The essay represents an accomplished writing performance.

Each score point contains language that describes different levels of quality for each of the three criteria. For example, on the criteria Development of Ideas, note the different levels of quality:

Criterion: Development of Ideas			
Score Point 1	**Score Point 2**	**Score Point 3**	**Score Point 4**
The development of ideas is weak. The essay is ineffective because the writer uses details and examples that are inappropriate, vague, or insufficient. The essay is insubstantial because the writer's response to the prompt is vague or confused. In some cases, the essay as a whole is only weakly linked to the prompt.	The development of ideas is minimal. The essay is superficial because the writer uses details and examples that are not always appropriate or are too briefly or partially presented. The essay reflects little or no thoughtfulness. The writer's response to the prompt is sometimes formulaic. The writer develops the essay in a manner that demonstrates only a limited understanding of the expository writing task.	The development of ideas is sufficient because the writer uses details and examples that are specific and appropriate, adding some substance to the essay. The essay reflects some thoughtfulness. The writer's response to the prompt is original rather than formulaic. The writer develops the essay in a manner that demonstrates a good understanding of the expository writing task.	The development of ideas is effective because the writer uses details and examples that are specific and well chosen, adding substance to the essay. The essay is thoughtful and engaging. The writer may choose to use his/her unique experiences or view of the world as a basis for writing or to connect ideas in interesting ways. The writer develops the essay in a manner that demonstrates a thorough understanding of the expository writing task.

If you wanted (or are compelled by the school) to use an analytic rubric to derive a number grade for assessing just the Development of Ideas criterion, it might look something like the following.

Criteria	10 points	20 points	30 points	40 points
Development of Ideas	The development of ideas is weak. The essay is ineffective because the writer uses details and examples that are inappropriate, vague, or insufficient.	The development of ideas is minimal. The essay is superficial because the writer uses details and examples that are not always appropriate or are too briefly or partially presented.	The development of ideas is sufficient because the writer uses details and examples that are specific and appropriate, adding some substance to the essay.	The development of ideas is effective because the writer uses details and examples that are specific and well chosen, adding substance to the essay.

Whether you choose to use a holistic rubric or an analytic rubric, you will need to identify the criteria for the assessment. In other words, what specific things do you expect to find in the final product, performance, or demonstration? If you have followed the principles recommended in chapter 6, that's pretty easy. The criteria are:

- Use and application of the definition of the concept

- Use and application of the critical attributes of the concept

- Use and application of examples and/or non-examples of the concept

- Thinking reflects at least the performance standard (the verb)

- Use and application includes one or more of the process skills

The assessment will depend on the particular use and application of the criteria to the products, performances, or demonstrations. Remember that the students must have practiced these uses and applications in the Students Do Something With the Stuff (right-hand box) in the same way that you are assessing them.

SUMMARY

- Students learn together (right hand box).

- They may be assessed individually.

- Traditional paper and pencil assessments (fill-in-the-blank, etc.) will only tell you about short-term retention of the content standard. They tell you virtually nothing about what the students can do with the content (the performance standard and the process skills).

- The summative and formative assessment must match. Whatever students did together in the right-hand box must match what they are asked to do independently in the bottom box.

- The summative assessment must produce a product, performance, or demonstration.

- The products, performances, or demonstrations may be assessed with either a holistic or an analytic rubric.

- For either kind of assessment, you must develop criteria on which the product, performance, or demonstration will be judged.

- Once you have identified the criteria, you must develop descriptive language that differentiates each score point.

- Assessment and grading are not necessarily the same thing.

Most teacher evaluation systems express expectations about student assessment. Obviously, you want to know and follow your district's expectations. As you begin to think about individual, summative assessment, ask yourself these questions:

- What happened (or did not happen) in the right-hand box (students doing something with the stuff) that tells me they are ready to be individually assessed? What input will I get from my students to tell me that they are ready to be individually assessed?

- How can I make certain that the summative assessment (bottom box) matches whatever students did together in the right-hand box?

- How can I go beyond (or perhaps even eliminate) traditional paper and pencil assessments (fill-in-the-blank, etc.)?

- What product, performance, or demonstration will individual students produce—not merely a paper and pencil test?

- What kind of scoring criteria and rubric will I design to assess individual student learning (the products, performances, or demonstrations)? What might be the impact on their learning if I give them the rubric in advance?

Descriptors from Texas Teacher Evaluation and Support System (T-TESS) Related to Student Assessment

From the T-TESS Scoring Guide

PLANNING DIMENSION 1.2 Data and Assessment: The teacher uses formal and informal methods to measure student progress, then manages and analyzes student data to inform instruction.

- Formal and informal assessments to monitor progress of all students and incorporate appropriate diagnostic, formative and summative assessments data into lesson plans.

- Substantive, specific and timely feedback to students, families and other school personnel on the growth of students in relation to classroom and campus goals, while maintaining student confidentiality.

- Analysis of student data connected to specific instructional strategies and use of results to reflect on his or her teaching and to monitor teaching strategies and behaviors in relation to student success.

INSTRUCTION DIMENSION 2.5 Monitor and Adjust: The teacher formally and informally collects, analyzes and uses student progress data and makes needed lesson adjustments.

- Consistently invites input from students in order to monitor and adjust instruction and activities.

- Adjusts instruction and activities to maintain student engagement.

- Monitors student behavior and responses for engagement and understanding.

Works Referenced

Brookhart, Susan M. (2013). *How to create and use rubrics for formative assessment and grading.* Association for Supervision and Curriculum Development, Alexandria, VA.

Sarah Goodwin, *What is "academic assessment"?* Skidmore College: Saratoga Springs, NY. Retrieved from https://www.skidmore.edu/assessment/faq/what-is-assessment.php

Mctighe, Jay; O'Connor, Ken (November 2005). "Seven practices for effective learning". *Educational Leadership.* 63 (3): 10–17.

Scriven, M. (1991, 4th Edition). *Evaluation thesaurus.* Newbury Park, CA: Sage Publications.

Texas Education Agency (2011). *STAAR, Grade 4 Expository Writing Rubric.* Austin, TX.

CHAPTER 8

LEARNING ENVIRONMENT AND CLASSROOM MANAGEMENT

One of your most critical tasks is creating a positive learning environment for your classroom while also establishing procedural and behavioral norms.

Learning Environment

The Glossary of Education Reform defines learning environment as follows:

(Learning environment) encompasses the culture of a school or class—its presiding ethos and characteristics, including how individuals interact with and treat one another—as well as the ways in which teachers may organize an educational setting to facilitate learning—e.g., by conducting classes in relevant natural ecosystems, grouping desks in specific ways, decorating the walls with learning materials, or utilizing audio, visual, and digital technologies. …

Educators may also argue that learning environments have both a direct and indirect influence on student learning, including their engagement in what is being taught, their motivation to learn, and their sense of well-being, belonging, and personal safety. For example, learning environments filled with sunlight and stimulating educational materials would likely be considered more conducive to learning than drab spaces without windows or decoration, as would schools with fewer incidences of misbehavior, disorder, bullying, and illegal activity. How adults interact with students and how students interact with one another may also be considered aspects of a learning environment, and phrases such as "positive learning environment" or "negative learning environment" are commonly used in reference to the social and emotional dimensions of a school or class.

Building trust and relationships is vital if learning is to occur. If your students trust you, they will work harder, be more committed to what you want them to do, and behave in more appropriate ways. In addition, if you work hard at building positive relationships with your students, they (and you) will be happier and more motivated to engage in learning activities.

How do you (and your students) recognize and respond to the learning environment?

Teacher and Student Behaviors Associated with Learning Environment

The table below identifies <u>teacher behaviors</u> associated with learning environment. The more of the behaviors on the left side that you exhibit, the more likely it is that you are creating a positive learning environment.

Positively Associated	Negatively Associated
Activities are interesting and maximize student participation	Activities are not interesting and have little student participation
Positive reinforcement of behavior	Extinction (ignoring appropriate student behavior)
Positive reinforcement of learning	Not providing positive reinforcement of learning
Correcting incorrect responses and preserving student dignity	Providing negative/demeaning corrective feedback
Patiently assisting students who are having difficulty	Ignoring or being impatient with students who are having difficulty
Using humor in a positive way to deal with a potentially negative/awkward situation (learning or behavior)	Using sarcasm/negative criticism in dealing with a potentially negative situation (learning or behavior)
Relating content/activity to students' interest or experience	Dull, routine, or boring content/activity
Communicating value or importance of content or activity	Not communicating value or importance of content or activity
Using student names	Not using student names
Giving specific feedback for correct/incorrect performance	Telling students they are wrong without telling them why
Applying rules/expectations positively, consistently, and fairly	Applying rules/expectations negatively, inconsistently, unfairly
Implementing instruction that is challenging while providing opportunities for students to be successful	Implementing instruction that is too difficult (too easy) for students to feel successful

Using positive/patient vocal tone	Using negative impatient vocal tone
High energy/enthusiasm, moving around, animated	Unenthusiastic/sedentary

The previous table was all about <u>you</u> and your behavior. The following table lists <u>student behaviors</u> associated with learning environment. If you see them exhibit the behaviors on the left, you are well on your way to creating a positive learning environment in your classroom. If you repeatedly see the student behaviors on the right, you should re-evaluate what you are doing or not doing.

Positively Associated	Negatively Associated
Students excited/eager	Students bored, lethargic
High level of voluntary student participation	Low level of voluntary student participation
Student-initiated contributions/extensions/ examples/discussion	Few student-initiated contributions/extensions/ examples/discussion
Students who are having difficulty continue to make effort	Students who are having difficulty quit or give up
Students appropriately question/challenge the teacher/each other	Students do not question/challenge the teacher/others appropriately
Students having difficulty are not reluctant to ask for assistance	Students having difficulty reluctant to ask for assistance
Students on-task/engaged with little direction/ manipulation by teacher	Students on-task/engaged primarily because of direction/manipulation by teacher

Routines and Procedures

As discussed above, creating a positive learning environment is an essential component of classroom management. To prevent problem behaviors in the classroom, it is often necessary for you to change your own behaviors.

An additional component of the learning environment is clear and effective routines and procedures. Catherine Kaiser defines these as

> … simply a set of procedures for handling both daily occurrences (e.g.,
> taking attendance, starting a class period, or turning in assignments). …
> Essentially, once taught, routines are daily activities that students are able
> to complete with little or no teacher assistance, which accomplishes two
> objectives: (a) students have more opportunity to learn and (b) teachers can
> devote more time to instruction. Establishing a consistent and predictable
> routine serves a number of classroom functions. For example, a routine helps
> to simplify a complex environment and inform students exactly what to
> expect, what is expected of them, and what acceptable behavior is. Routines

allow students to quickly accomplish day-to-day tasks that are required of both the teacher and students. Routines also help to create smoother transitions between activities and therefore allow fewer opportunities for disruptions to occur. In addition, when students are expected to complete routine tasks, they have the opportunity to learn greater responsibility and more self-management....

Teachers should identify recurring and predictable classroom events:

- Administrative Procedures: storing personal and instructional materials; using the restroom; taking attendance; making announcements; turning in work; and dismissing students to go to another classroom, the playground, or home.

- Instructional Tasks: getting every student's attention for instruction; ensuring that students behave in ways that maximize positive outcomes during teacher-led instruction or group-learning settings (not interrupting you or other students, not shouting out answers, "edge of table voices" during group work, etc.); handing in or returning student work.

- Interactive Routines: how to participate in discussions, behaving as expected in groups, and following rules for getting the teacher's attention.

A Note on Students from Poverty

Unfortunately, our society is characterized by increasingly large numbers of economically disadvantaged students. Note that the distinction here is on poverty/class and not on race/ethnicity. One of the mistakes you want to avoid is taking for granted that your students come hard-wired with the social skills and values you want to see. They may or may not come to school with a concrete understanding of behaviors and their predictable consequences. Dunbar and Maeroff refer to this as "social capital."

They suggest that children of poverty, especially generational poverty, often are lacking in four types of social capital:

1. *A sense of academic initiative.* Many students lack a school work ethic, good study habits, and a high level of self-discipline. Academic success is not perceived as relevant to their future lives.

2. *A sense of knowing.* Many students do not have a sturdy foundation upon which to build success in school. They do not have the opportunities to thrive, which include pre-school attendance, travel, summer camps, home computers, tutors, music lessons, organized sports, exposure to the arts, coaching for college admissions tests, and visits to colleges.

3. *A sense of connectedness.* Many students feel alienated and do not have a sense of belonging to their community, neighborhood, or school. To be successful in school, students must feel that they "belong" and perceive the work of school as having great value. Connectedness also means that students have good relationships with adults in the school, the home, and the neighborhood. These adults can be advocates for students as they face barriers and problems in and out of school.

4. *A sense of well-being.* Poverty, concerns for one's emotional and psychological well-being, and worries about what the future holds cause many students to develop a negative sense of well-being. As a result, many have little sense of hope combined with low levels of self-confidence and self-respect.

Ruby Payne differentiates between generational poverty and situational poverty: "Generational poverty and situational poverty are different. Generational poverty is defined as being in poverty for two generations or longer. Situational poverty involves a shorter time and is caused by circumstance, i.e., death, illness, divorce." Payne has at times been criticized regarding some of her generalizations about children of poverty. I offer a few of her insights about what she calls the "hidden rules" that govern behavior for your own analysis and evaluation.

Generational Poverty	Middle Class
The driving forces for decision making are survival, relationships, and entertainment.	The driving forces for decision making are work and achievement.
Physical fighting is how conflict is resolved. If you only know casual register, you do not have the words to negotiate a resolution. Respect is accorded to those who can physically defend themselves.	Fighting is done verbally. Physical fighting is viewed with distaste.
Destiny and fate govern. The notion of having choices is foreign. Discipline is about penance and forgiveness, not change.	Discipline is about changing behavior. To stay in the middle class, one must be self-governing and self-supporting. A reprimand is taken seriously (at least the pretense is there), without smiling, and with some deference to authority.

Classroom Behavior Norms

If your students do not bring with them the behaviors, attitudes, and interpersonal skills that you want in your classroom, you must <u>teach</u> them. You may need to intentionally teach each procedure and what is expected of their behavior. Plan to review and reteach as frequently as necessary and to communicate to students the importance of each procedure or behavior.

Discuss with your students the importance of classroom norms. Invite students to create procedures with you. This process can nurture a sense of ownership in the norms and in your classroom. Remind students that these norms are for you as well as for them. Include a discussion of logical consequences with students during this discussion to focus on possible consequences if one of these "classroom norms" is violated (modeling for students and teacher).

Keep the norms to a minimum. The more rules you have, the more valuable instructional time you may spend enforcing them! Make sure that the norms are necessary for all your students. Kaser suggests that "(t)he repeated failure of one student to demonstrate the expected behavior may suggest to the teacher one course of action; however, if the teacher observes that multiple students do not successfully engage in that behavior, that is a clear signal that a different response is called for." Make sure the norms address <u>expected behavior</u> rather than a "do not…" format. The details of those norms will emerge as you intentionally teach the norms and review them as necessary. Here is a sample of what those norms may look like. Note that they all begin with *we*—you are committing yourself to the norms that you expect from your students.

Norms

- We will respect ourselves and others.
- We will put forth our best effort at all times.
- We will be prepared for class each day.
- We will follow directions when given.
- We will pay attention, participate, and ask questions.
- We will speak to others in a courteous and respectful way.
- We will take responsibility for our actions.

Shalaway suggests the following as a starting point and expanding it to meet the needs of your class and grade level.

1. Treat others as you would like to be treated.

2. Respect other people and their property (e.g., no hitting, no stealing).

3. Laugh with anyone, but laugh at no one.

4. Be responsible for your own learning.

5. Come to class and hand in assignments on time.

6. Do not disturb people who are working.

David Tow takes a much broader view of norms in a high school classroom. He suggests taking classroom time to discuss the norms of society as a whole—the behaviors and attitudes that are critical for success in the world beyond the classroom. Initially he was skeptical of the approach.

> "When I first opted for this method, I didn't really think it would work. I imagined it as an interesting experiment. But it did work. Not just with my high-performing debate kids or my AP English classes, but with all of them. My students who were burned out and checked out. Those who coasted by with Cs. Freshmen and seniors. Even my English language development students, many of whom have been in the country for less than six months, bought in to the method and grew. They all wanted to feel that their contributions mattered to the community. And if this alternative approach can at least prepare them for a more open, more pluralistic society, then I will take the time and energy it requires from me. That would be a worthy return on investment."

When Tow posts norms for his classroom, he includes a rationale for them that form the foundation for his on-going conversations with his students.

1. Be respectful to *yourself* because it sets the context for being able to participate in a community; to *others* because it is hard to be a student and everyone's struggles merit your respect; and to *the teacher* because although it is a position of authority, the teacher should also be vulnerable and learning.

2. Be engaged, because merely being present in the classroom does not necessarily qualify as participation, and a truly pluralistic community requires all voices.

3. Be prepared, because informed conversation requires prepared members, and preparation transcends just the work that is assigned—and is closer to deep thought, sincere skepticism, and a general willingness to interrogate assumptions.

4. Be courageous, because learning requires acknowledging that there are things we don't know, skills we lack, and ways in which we might still be foolish—which is a scary prospect for everyone in the class, teacher included.

Consequences

There is a difference between punishment and logical consequences. Consider appropriate and logical consequences for students who follow or fail to follow classroom norms and communicate both sets of consequences. Your nonnegotiable mantra should be that consequences for failure to abide by classroom norms will never, ever publicly demean, embarrass, or humiliate. So, forget putting names on the board, "pulling colors," and other such consequences. The Center for Responsive Classrooms makes these distinctions between punishment and logical consequences:

- While effective in stopping the misbehavior of the moment, punishment does little to increase student responsibility.

- Punishment often leads to feelings of anger, discouragement, and resentment, and an increase in evasion and deception.

The goal of logical consequences is to help children develop internal understanding, self-control, and a desire to follow the rules.

- Logical consequences help children look more closely at their behaviors and consider the results of their choices.

- Unlike punishment, where the intention is to make a child feel shamed, the intention of logical consequences is to help children develop internal controls and to learn from their mistakes in a supportive atmosphere.

Logical consequences are respectful of the child's dignity while punishment often calls upon an element of shame.

- Logical consequences respond to the misbehavior in ways that preserve the dignity of the child. The message is that the behavior is a problem, not that the child is a problem.

- The teacher's tone of voice is critical in distinguishing logical consequences from punishment. There are many ways to say to a child that they've spilled their juice and should clean it up. If the tone is angry or punitive, then it's no longer a logical consequence.

- The same consequence can be respectful in one situation and demeaning in another. Mopping the floor is a respectful consequence for the child who chooses to have a water fight at the drinking fountain, but not for the child who fails to complete his work.

Logical consequences are related to the child's behavior; punishment usually is not.

- Leaving the group is related to being disruptive in a group; missing recess is not. Cleaning up graffiti on the bathroom wall is related to drawing the graffiti on the wall; being suspended from school is not.

- Logical consequences require that the teacher gather more information before reacting. The teacher takes time to assess the situation and determine, often with input from the child, what will help fix the problem.

- The belief underlying the use of logical consequences is that with reflection and practice children will want to do better, whereas the belief behind punishment is that children will do better only because they fear punishment and will seek to avoid it.

- Teachers using logical consequences begin with a belief in the basic goodness of children and the knowledge that every child is a learner, struggling to establish meaningful relationships with us, each other, and the school community.

- These teachers expect that all children will from time to time lose their control and make mistakes.

- The use of logical consequences helps children fix their mistakes and know what to do next time.

Teachers frequently ask, "Is it ever okay for a child to feel bad about his/her behavior?" Of course it is. When children misbehave, chances are they already feel bad. Our job is not to make them feel worse but to help them choose a better course of action the next time.

Teacher Magazine offers these examples of logical consequences:

- **You break it, you fix it** can be used to mend emotional messes as well as physical messes. A child can rebuild a block tower after accidentally knocking it over. A student can repair hurt feelings with an apology or action. An apology or action may be doing something to soothe the injury, such as drawing a picture or playing a game.

- **Temporary loss of privilege** is a simple way to help a student remember to use that privilege (art materials, recess, group time) responsibly. Losing a privilege for a class period or a day can help a child pause to remember or relearn a rule.

- **Time-out or "take a break"** is a strategy to help students learn self-control. A student who is disrupting the work of the group is asked to leave for a few minutes. Give the student a chance to regain composure and rejoin the group on his or her own.

Summary

- A positive learning environment is essential if you want your students to be engaged, motivated risk-takers.

- If you monitor your own behavior, you can evaluate whether or not you are doing those things that create a positive or negative learning environment.

- If you monitor your students' behavior, you can evaluate whether they perceive the learning environment as positive or negative.

- You must establish clear, predictable, and consistent procedures and routines if you want the foundation for a well-managed classroom.

- Some students may come to you already hard-wired to absorb and follow procedures and routines. In addition, they may bring with them the social capital/skills and will quickly conform to the behavioral norms and consequences of your classroom.

- Many students may come from a background of generational poverty. These students may not have the social capital/skills that you want. If not, you must intentionally plan lessons to teach the procedures, routines, and behavior norms and help students understand their importance,

- Err on the side of a short list of behavior norms; you can always add to the list if you need to.

- Consequences of failure to meet the norms should be logical and must never publicly demean or embarrass anyone.

- The best classroom management tools in your kit are lessons that are interesting, engaging, and relevant.

Most teacher evaluation systems express expectations about classroom management and learning environment. Obviously, you want to know and follow your district's expectations. As you begin to think about individual, summative assessment ask yourself these questions:

- What processes and procedures can I put in place that maximize:
  - a safe, accessible, and efficient classroom?

  - the clarity and efficiency of all procedures, routines, and transitions?

  - student actively participation in groups, management of supplies and equipment with very limited direction from me?

- How can I monitor my own behavior to make certain that I am applying expectations for behavior effectively, efficiently, and consistently?

- As I design the lesson, what decisions am I making to engage all students in relevant, meaningful learning?

- How will I monitor students at all times to insure that they are communicating me and their peers at all times?

- How will I monitor my own behavior to ensure that I am exhibiting those behaviors that build trust and create a positive learning environment?

- How will I monitor the behavior of my students to determine whether or not they perceive that there is a trusting, positive learning environment?

- Based on the unique needs and experiences of my students, what classroom and social behaviors do I anticipate that I will have to intentionally teach them?

Descriptors from Texas Teacher Evaluation and Support System (T-TESS) Related to Learning Environment and Classroom Management

From the T-TESS Scoring Guide

3.1 Learning Environment: Classroom Environment, Routines and Procedures

- The teacher organizes a safe, accessible and efficient classroom.

- All procedures, routines and transitions are clear and efficient.

- Students actively participate in groups, manage supplies and equipment with very limited teacher direction.

- The classroom is safe and organized to support learning objectives and is accessible.

3.2 Learning Environment: Managing Student Behavior

- Consistently implements the campus and/or classroom behavior system proficiently.

- Most students meet expected classroom behavior standards.

3.3 Learning Environment: Classroom Culture

- Engages all students in relevant, meaningful learning.

- Students work respectfully individually and in groups.

Works Referenced

Abbott, Steven (Ed.), (2014, August 26). "Hidden curriculum." *The glossary of education reform.* Retrieved from http://edglossary.org/hidden-curriculum

Findley, Todd. (December 15, 2015). *Teaching strategies: 22 powerful closures.* Retrieved from https://www.edutopia.org/blog/22-powerful-closure-activities-todd-finley

Kaser, Catherine Hoffman (2014). *Series on highly effective practices: Classroom routines.* Retrieved from https://www.odu.edu/content/dam/odu/col-dept/cdse/docs/4-classroom-routines.pdf

Maeroff, G. I. (1998, February). "Altered destinies: Making life better for children in need." *Phi Delta Kappan*, 79. Retrieved from https://msu.edu/~dunbarc/dunbar3.pdf

Payne, Ruby K. (1996. March). "Hidden rules." *Instructional Leader* Retrieved from http://homepages.wmich.edu/~ljohnson/Payne.pdf

Payne, Ruby K. (1913) *A framework for understanding poverty; a cognitive process.*

aha! Process, Inc. Highlands, Texas.

Responsive Classroom Newsletter (August 1998). Turner Falls, MA. Retrieved from https://www.responsiveclassroom.org/punishment-vs-logical-consequences/

Shalaway, Linda (2005). *Learning to teach...not just for beginners: the essential guide for all teachers.* Scholastic: New York.

Teacher. (2008) "What to do when kids break the rules." Retrieved from https://www.scholastic.com/teachers/articles/teaching-content/what-do-when-kids-break-rules/

Tow, David (October 11, 2017). *Why I don't have classroom rules.* Edutopia.org; George Lucas Educational Foundation"). Retrieved on December 12, 2017 from https://www.edutopia.org/article/why-i-dont-have-classroom-rules

EFFECTIVE TEACHING PRACTICES

Now that I have addressed curriculum, lesson design, and classroom management, this chapter will briefly highlight some of the common teaching strategies that you will likely use.

- Daily Closure
- Questioning Strategies
- Feedback
- Retention and Transfer of Learning

Daily Closure

Remember that the greatest misunderstanding of the Redneck Lesson Cycle is that it describes an instructional period. It does not. It reflects the major components of a lesson from the time you begin teaching a curriculum objective to the time you have completed summative assessment. For low-level procedural knowledge, that might be one class period. For more complex conceptual knowledge, you will probably need multiple days/class periods.

Instead of a bell ending the instructional time, some brief activity that draws significant portions of the lesson together adds value.

There are several advantages to a daily lesson closure:

- Check for understanding and inform subsequent instruction
- Emphasize key information

- Tie up loose ends

- Correct misunderstanding

- Summarize, review, and demonstrate their understanding of major points

- Consolidate and internalize key information

- Link lesson ideas to a conceptual framework and/or previously-learned knowledge

- Transfer ideas to new situations

Closure activity options range from the mundane to the creative.

Summary Closure: Ask the students to summarize the key elements of the lesson.

Value Closure: Ask students to identify at least one element of the lesson that they found valuable or interesting.

Todd Findley offers twenty-two creative closure activities. Among them are:

- Snowstorm: Students write down what they learned on a piece of scratch paper and wad it up. Given a signal, they throw their paper snowballs in the air. Then each learner picks up a nearby response and reads it aloud.

- Parent Hotline: Give students an interesting question about the lesson without further discussion. Email their guardians the question so that the topic can be discussed over dinner.

- DJ Summary: Learners write what they learned in the form of a favorite song.

- Gallery Walk: On chart paper, small groups of students write and draw what they learned. After the completed works are attached to the classroom walls, other students affix Stickies to the posters to extend on the ideas, add questions, or offer praise.

- Cover It: Have kids sketch a book cover. The title is the class topic. The author is the student. A short celebrity endorsement or blurb should summarize and articulate the lesson's benefits.

- So what? What takeaways from the lesson will be important to know three years from now? Why?

- Beat the Clock: Ask a question. Give students ten seconds to confer with peers before you call on a random student to answer. Repeat.

- Review It: Direct kids to raise their hands if they can answer your questions. Classmates agree (thumbs up) or disagree (thumbs down) with the response.

- Simile Me: Have students complete the following sentence: "The [concept, skill, word] is like _____ because _____."

- Exit Ticket Folder: Ask students to write their name, what they learned, and any lingering questions on a blank card or "ticket." Before they leave class, direct them to deposit their exit tickets in a folder or bin labeled either

- ◦ Stop (I'm totally confused.)
- ◦ Go (I'm ready to move on.)
- ◦ Proceed with caution (I could use some clarification on . . .)

Questioning Strategies

Can you imagine trying to teach without asking your students questions? Questioning strategies are among the most important tools in your tool kit. Questioning keeps students engaged and participating and helps you check for understanding.

When you are a skilled questioner, students tend to become more active learners and think more deeply as they develop and organize their responses. Your questions have the potential to arouse their curiosity, to ponder or reflect about something. When students sit and listen to a teacher lecture, they are passive learners. When students are participating there is greater potential that they will retain what they learn. Passive learners may comprehend information in the short term, but to retain it they must feel motivated to apply the information or connect it to previous knowledge.

While the psychological and brain research are rich with advice on questioning, I will focus on some of the basic strategies.

- Ask questions to pairs/triads/quads rather than to individuals.
  Rationale: This strategy maximizes student engagement and participation. Additionally, it places students in a position to assist each other—sometimes students can explain a complex answer more effectively than you can! It builds the culture of your classroom into a "we" not "me" environment in which students are interdependent. Be sure to provide wait time for them to think and orally process the answer.

- Ask the question first; then call on the student(s).
  Rationale: When you ask a question, you want <u>all</u> of your students to be thinking about the question and answer. If you call on a student and then ask a question, only that student may be thinking about the question/answer. You are unintentionally sending a signal that only the student called on needs to be thinking; you want them <u>all</u> thinking! Be careful not to allow one or two students to dominate.

- Provide 3-5 seconds of "wait time" between asking the question and calling on a student.
  Rationale: Typically, teachers wait less than one second between asking a question and calling on a student! If you ask the question and immediately call on a student,

no one has time to really think about the answer. Wait time increases the likelihood that more students will engage in thinking about the question. Silence creates what Madeline Hunter referred as level of tension or level of concern. By asking the question and waiting 3-5 seconds, you raise the level of tension/concern. In the silence, students may be thinking: "Whoa—the teacher may call on me, so maybe I need to be thinking about what my answer will be!"

- Avoid answering your own question.
  Rationale: Do teachers really do that? Yep. This happens most often when you ask a question and students do not immediately volunteer or respond. Without realizing it, you are sending a covert message to your students: "When I ask a question and you do not want to think about it, just sit there—you do not have to think. Eventually I will answer the questions myself."

- Avoid volunteerism.
  Rationale: When you primarily call on students who volunteer, you are unintentionally sending another covert message to your students: "If you would like to engage and think, you may signal me of your desire by raising your hands. If you would prefer NOT to engage and think, you can signal me of your wishes by not raising your hand. In that case I will not call on you." Crazy, isn't it? Consider eliminating hand raising altogether. Establish a procedure in which you ask a question, wait 3-5 seconds, and then call a student at random. In that way, everyone has the incentive to remain engaged and think—they never know where the lightning might strike!

- Avoid asking "yes or no" questions. These questions do little to promote thinking; plus, they have a 50% chance of just guessing the correct answer.

- Be aware of the tone of your questioning.
  Rationale: Are you asking questions in a friendly, relaxed manner or do you sound like a prosecuting attorney? Make questioning a conversation and not an interrogation. How you question and respond influences the climate/learning environment—positively or negatively.

- Listen carefully when students are responding.
  Rationale: Even when they do not know the answer, their response may provide insight into where their misunderstanding occurred, giving you the opportunity to clarify or to build on a partially correct answer. When their answers are correct, you are able to give them <u>specific</u> feedback on why their answers were correct.

- As a classroom norm, allow students to "pass" perhaps no more than one time during a lesson. This has the potential of creating a zone of safety.

- Ask fewer convergent (closed) questions and more divergent (open) questions.
  Rationale: Convergent questions have only one correct answer. Divergent questions have more than one possible correct answer. Convergent questions tend to be at

the lower level of Bloom's Taxonomy of Cognitive Learning (Know/Understand). Divergent questions tend to be at the higher levels of the taxonomy (analyze, evaluate, synthesize)—so called "higher-ordered" questions. Convergent questions do not require much thinking; they merely require recall of isolated information. Divergent questions have greater potential to cause students to make connections and play with the information. Plus, they are much more interesting and engaging.

- Plan a half-dozen key questions.
  Rationale: Planning key questions is an essential part of planning a lesson. While most questions will be intuitive and dependent on the needs of the moment, you need to have a sense of where you are going with the lesson. Try to scaffold/spiral the questions so that they unfold in a logical sequence toward the most important learning. When students are working together, plan questions to ask each group. Some of these questions may simply check for understanding. Others should be questions that elicit the key learning that you want to occur.

Formative Feedback During Learning

Positive Feedback/Reinforcement

Behavioral psychologists like B. F. Skinner argue that a behavior followed by positive reinforcement increases the likelihood that that the behavior will occur again. Humanistic psychologists like Abraham Maslow and Carl Rogers argue for the affective effect of reinforcement—helping people feel good and confident about their behavior is also a legitimate outcome of positive reinforcement. The works of Skinner, Rogers, and Maslow are great resources if you want to dig deeper into the psychology behind reinforcement theory.

The Spectrum Intervention Group, a Canadian organization that works with autistic students, offers the following rationale for providing positive feedback.

- It can (though does not always) serve as reinforcement, thus increasing the future rate of behavior that you are commenting on.

- It helps to build and maintain a positive rapport between you and your learner.

- A history of positive feedback can generate motivation to engage in behavior that has contacted positive feedback in the past.

- It can lead to an increase in receptivity to future feedback (both positive and corrective).

- It can promote self-awareness, self-confidence and performance within certain situations

There is a difference between recognizing and praising. Think of a continuum of intensity that ranges from simple acknowledgement to lavish praise.

Acknowledge   Lavish Praise

That's correct.   *Great, thoughtful answer.*

Acknowledgement may be as simple as "That's correct" or "That's what I was looking for." Praise may be more elaborate: "That a very insightful answer" or "Great thinking." Madeline Hunter offered what she called the three S's of positive reinforcement.

- Swift: The reinforcement for appropriate behavior and successful learning should occur as soon as possible. Usually, the reinforcement should be immediately after the behavior. For written work or projects, the reinforcement may come later.

- Specific: Simply saying, "That's correct" may make the student feel good, but it does not necessarily tell the student <u>why</u> the behavior or learning was correct. Something like "That's a good answer because…." An even better approach might be "That's correct—someone tell us <u>why or how</u> it's correct" or "That's a reasonable interpretation—someone tell us why it's reasonable." This encourages your students to do the thinking and increases student participation.

- Sincere: Sincerity is typically based on a reasonable relationship between the quality of the behavior and the intensity of the teacher's response. For low level responses, a "That's correct" may be all that's necessary. For responses that represent deep or divergent thinking, consider more lavish words: "That is a really thoughtful answer" or "I would have never thought of that. How/why did you arrive at that conclusion?". Sometimes a correct response is low level, but it comes from a student who struggles and is rarely successful. In that case, bump your reinforcement up the continuum. Try to avoid getting in the "Very good" rut. I have been in classrooms where the teacher said "Very good" a dozen times in ten minutes. After a while, this just becomes verbal noise and has no impact on the students.

Corrective Feedback

When students are not being successful, you must provide corrective feedback; otherwise, they are unlikely to understand why they are not successful. This is one of the most difficult teaching skills to master. You are legitimately concerned that you may negatively impact their motivation and self-confidence and "make them feel dumb." However, if you do not give corrective feedback, students may experience <u>more</u> frustration and failure—they are wrong, but they have no idea what they need to do to get to right!

Recall the discussion in Chapter 3 of Bloom's Taxonomy of Cognitive Learning. Lower-level questions (Remember and Understand) are the most difficult for you to provide corrective feedback. These questions are known as <u>convergent questions</u>: there is only one correct answer. Suppose you ask, 'Who was the first President of the United States?" and the student responds "Thomas Jefferson." Thankfully, there are a few options.

- When a student gives you an incorrect response to a low-level question, the student doesn't know the answer to the question you asked and doesn't know the question to the answer he/she gave! Every incorrect answer is the answer to <u>some</u> question. So give the student the question to the answer he/she gave: "If I asked you who was the <u>third</u> President, you'd be correct. I'm looking for the first President." The student knows <u>something</u>—just not the answer to the question you asked!

- Take responsibility for the student's incorrect response. You are an adult, and you can tolerate the ego-strain! "I must not have been very clear when I presented this information earlier. Let me start over."

- Prompt at least one time. "Our first President was also known as the Father of Our Country and was the commander of the Revolutionary Army." or "Close your eyes— his picture is on the $1 bill."

Your tool kit of providing corrective feedback increases greatly when you are asking higher-level questions (Apply, Analyze, Evaluate, Create). These questions are known as <u>divergent questions</u>: there is more than one possible correct answer. That provides you with much more flexibility in providing corrective feedback. With divergent questions, you have the opportunity to probe and deepen student thinking—not just a "correct" answer.

- Probe the student's thinking:
  - Why are you thinking that's the correct answer?
  - Think out loud about how you came to that conclusion?
  - When you drew that conclusion, what information did you consider/reject?

- Provide scaffolded assistance by doing a mini-teach:
  - If you were to consider (*you provide some additional information*), how would that affect your conclusion?
  - When you drew your conclusion, how did you include (*you provide some additional information*)?
  - If I told you (*you provide some additional information*), how would you alter your conclusion?

- Ask for/give examples:
  - Give me an example of what you are describing/concluding.

- ◦ You said _____. How would that apply to (give an example)?

- • Involve other students:

  - ◦ Ask another student: Did you come to the same conclusion? Why/why not?

  - ◦ To the student with the incorrect response: Who would you like to call on for some feedback/a reaction to your answer?

- • Take responsibility for the student's incorrect response. As I indicated earlier, you are an adult, and your ego can take the hit! "I must not have been very clear when I presented this information earlier. Let me start over."

Whether you are asking convergent or divergent questions, students must ultimately know if they are successful or unsuccessful. Your challenge is to make sure that you always provide feedback in ways that do not demean or embarrass.

Be aware of your non-verbals—volume, pitch, tone, inflection, facial expressions, etc. Your words may be positive and respectful, but your non-verbals may send a contradictory message. Here's an example of how inflection alone can completely change your message. Read these out loud so that you can hear the difference.

I didn't say that you were wrong.

I **didn't** say that you were wrong.

I didn't **say** that you were wrong.

I didn't say that **you** were wrong.

I didn't say that you were **wrong**.

Retention and Transfer of Learning

Let's start out with working definitions of retention and transfer. Retention is the ability to remember things easily or for a long time. Baldwin and Ford define transfer as follows: "Learning or transfer of knowledge or transfer refers to learning in one context and applying it to another, i.e. the capacity to apply acquired knowledge and skills to new situations." Simons suggests that "There are three kids of transfer: from prior knowledge to learning, from learning to new learning, (and) from learning to application."

Retention of Learning

The National Training Laboratories has developed what they refer to as a Learning Pyramid which illustrates the percentage of retention associated with different teaching/learning strategies.

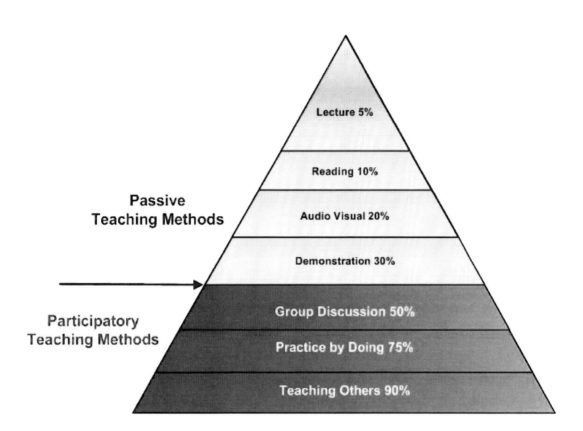

While there is some disagreement among scholars as to the accuracy of the percentages, the basic principles on which they are based are sound. In other words, if you teach others what you know, you will retain more of the knowledge.

Of particular note is the conclusion that the more students are participants in the learning, the more they will retain. Conversely, if the students are passive recipients of learning, the less likely it is that they will retain it.

At this point, connect these three things from previous chapters:

1. In the Redneck Lesson Cycle, I described the right-hand side box as "students doing something with the stuff (knowledge)."

2. In the Participatory Teaching Methods of The Learning Pyramid, students would typically be at the higher levels on Bloom's Taxonomy of Cognitive (Apply, Analyze, Evaluate, Create).

3. The Inductive Model of Teaching/Learning is a Participatory Teaching Method.

Recall the definition of Knowledge level learning—the lowest level of Bloom's Taxonomy of Cognitive Learning: retrieving information from <u>long-term memory</u>.

Advances in neuroscience are helping us understand why the brain retains or does not retain information. David Rock is a writer who has helped non-neuroscientists understand the brain research. For example, the brain is particularly sensitive to emotions: "(P)ositive emotions (such as) interest, happiness, joy and desire are approach emotions. This state is one of increased dopamine levels (in the brain), important for interest and learning." Frederickson summarizes a large body of research that suggests "… that people experiencing positive emotions perceive more options when trying to solve problems, solve more non-linear problems that require insight (Jung-Beeman, 2007), collaborate better and generally perform better overall. The opposite is also true. When the brain experiences negative emotions (fear, criticism, unpredictability, attack, unfairness), the level of dopamine in the brain decreases and impairs the brain's ability to function at its greatest potential."

When the brain acquires new knowledge, it physically creates something call a *dendrite*. Collins *Dictionary of Medicine* defines a dendrite as "one of the usually numerous branches of a nerve cell that carry impulses toward the cell body." These electrical impulses create "… the most complex interconnection between nerve cells … so that elaborate control arrangements over the passage of nerve impulses are made possible." Really clear, right?

The international organization Envision offers an explanation that is a bit more learner-friendly.

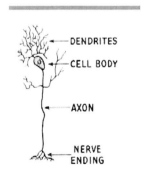

You are born with at least 100 billion brain cells, called **neurons**. As you listen to, talk about, or practice something, fibers called **dendrites** grow out of your neurons. Learning is built, as your network of dendrites grow higher and higher, with new dendrites sprouting from existing dendrites. In other words, your brain is building new knowledge upon the things you already know (like a tree sprouting twigs from existing branches).

These new dendrites are "excited"—they are moving around in the brain. The brain automatically wants to connect the new dendrite (learning) to dendrites that represent prior learning and experience—the brain is attempting to make sense out of the new learning. If the new dendrite/learning cannot make a connection to prior learning/experience, it is unlikely to be retained and recalled later—short-term vs. long-term memory.

When two dendrites grow close together, they have the ability to connect. The small gap at the contact point is called the *synapse*.

Hestwood and Russell explain the phenomenon this way:

Special chemicals called neurotransmitters (dopamine, endorphins) carry the electrical signals across the synapse. As the dendrites make more and more connections, they grow thicker with a fatty coating of myelin. The thicker the dendrites, the faster the signals travel. Faster, stronger, double connections last a very long time. You remember what you learned!

New dendrites can only grow off of what is already there. New skills must connect to and grow off previously learned skills. If you do not have the necessary dendrites in place, new material will seem to go "right over your head."

The amygdala processes F.A.S.T emotions (Fear, Anxiety, Stress, and Threat). The prefrontal cortex is where your higher order thinking skills get processed. If amygdala activity is low, the prefrontal cortex activity is high. If amygdala activity is high, the prefrontal cortex activity is low. Why?

F.A.S.T emotions flood your body with adrenaline. Adrenaline makes it hard for the neurotransmitters to carry messages across the synapses in your brain. Your brain goes into "freeze, flight, or fight" mode.

Endorphins make you feel calm. If you are calm, your amygdala activity is low so your prefrontal activity is high. Your body produces endorphins when you relax, exercise, laugh, or learn new things.

There are at least two critical messages here.

1. Recall the discussion of learning environment and learning climate in Chapter 8. When the learning environment is emotionally/psychologically safe, stress-free, happy, joyful, and relevant, the brain is producing the chemicals necessary to retain learning and to think. When the learning environment is emotionally/psychologically unsafe, fearful, boring, and irrelevant, the brain is <u>not</u> producing the chemicals that allow it to retain and think.

2. If dendrites can grow and connect, the potential for long-term retention and deep thinking increases. The ideal point in your lesson for this to happen is on the right-hand side of the Redneck Lesson Cycle where students are Doing Something With the Stuff. If the majority of time is spent on the top with Students Getting Stuff, the

likelihood of the new learning going into long-term memory (retention), is minimal. In a dull, inactive lesson, there just are not sufficient opportunities for every student's brain to make connections by growing/connecting the dendrites. From Learning to Application is the whole point of the right-hand box. Recall from Chapter 5 that students will be "verbing the stuff" and marrying process skills to the stuff. In doing that, there should be positive transfer and greater retention from their having learned the stuff on the top row to doing something with the stuff on the right-hand side.

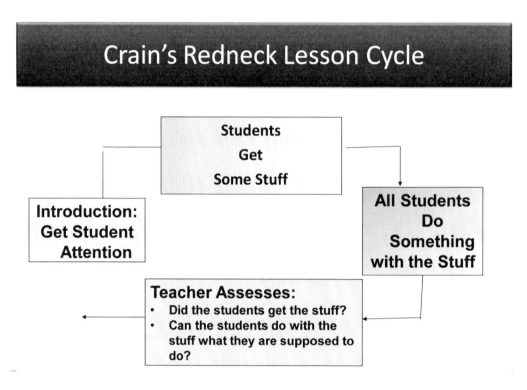

Finally, recall the scoring rubric for the Texas Teacher Evaluation and Support system (T-TESS). The continuum of scoring ranges from teacher-centered instruction on the low end of the continuum to student-centered instruction on the high end of the continuum.

Transfer of Learning

There are two kinds of transfer: positive and negative. Positive transfer occurs when old learning/experiences <u>assist</u> with acquisition of new leaning. Here are some examples of positive transfer:

- When students understand the <u>concepts</u> of addition and subtraction, it may help them understand the inverse operations of multiplication and division.

- Learning to play badminton may help an individual learn to play ping pong.

- If students understand the elements of plot in fiction, it may help them learn the elements of plot in biography and autobiography—they share some elements, but not others.

- Learning the critical attributes of *revolution* will likely help them learn about <u>any</u> revolution.

- When students understand the critical attributes of *ecosystem*, it will help them understand <u>any</u> ecosystem they encounter.

Sometimes, prior learning and experience may interfere in the acquisition of new learning—negative transfer. Imagine yourself moving to Great Britain where the steering wheel of a car is on the right-hand side and you drive on the left-hand side of the road! I recall observing in a classroom where the teacher asked a student to name the seasons. The student's response was "hunting and fishing!" Every discipline has common misconceptions that students may bring with them to your classroom. If your school uses the curriculum documents from the Texas Resource System (formerly known as C-SCOPE), they identify those misconceptions for each unit. The following are some examples of possible negative transfer of learning:

In mathematics, there are some common student misconceptions in working with integers:

- The negative sign (-) always means subtraction.

- Subtraction means the larger number always goes first.

- If the problem begins with a negative, the answer will be negative.

- Confusing magnitude for negative numbers. For example, which is bigger -8 or -5?

- Focusing on procedures, and the use of expressions such as "owning" when the quantity is positive and "owing" when the quantity negative, seems to result in numerous student misconceptions in working with integers.

- Students with knowledge of integers based in procedures seem to be able to handle addition and subtraction with integers following rules, but misconceptions of the procedures become apparent when they begin multiplication and division.

Some of the science concepts that cause the most headaches for teachers:

- Students struggle because they can't seem to grasp that a heavy object does not fall faster than a small object. No, an object falls to the earth at the same rate regardless of their mass.

- Blood inside the body is red. No, blood inside the body is blue. Blood only becomes red when it comes into contact with the air (oxygenated blood).

Students have many misconceptions that are reflected in their writing:

- They use commas following the "as the spirit moves" rule: "it just sounds like you need one." Another issue is that they somehow believe that they should put a comma in front of a conjunction even when it's only a compound verb.

- You can't start a sentence with the words "but" or "because." But of course you can, particularly when it's about creating voice and emphasis.

State assessment data in social studies indicate that many students bring misconceptions that interfere with their learning about the system of limited government in the United States Constitution.

- They think *republicanism* is a political party.

- They are confused about the difference between *checks and balances* and *separation of powers*.

- And they believe that *individual rights* are whatever <u>they</u> think are their rights—not helpful when you are teaching eighth graders!

At the beginning of this section of the chapter, I pointed out that Simons suggests that there are three kinds of positive transfer:

- from prior knowledge to learning,

- from learning to new learning, and

- from learning to application.

Let me amplify that a bit.

- Positive Transfer from Prior Knowledge to Learning: This type of transfer is probably the most common kind of positive transfer. Students bring with them a set of prior learning and experiences (sometimes referred to as their *schema*). This learning may or may not have occurred in a formal school setting. Suppose you are teaching about the differences between the Senate and the House of Representatives. The student who has visited the United States Capitol and seen the two legislative chambers with a tour guide has some prior knowledge about the differences and has a visual image of 435 seats in the U.S. House of Representatives and one hundred desks in the United States Senate. A student who has visited the Grand Canyon already has a visual image when you begin to teach about erosion on the surface of the earth. In school, the concept of algebraic thinking begins in the primary grade levels: "Algebraic reasoning. The student applies mathematical process standards to identify and apply number patterns within properties of numbers and operations in order to describe relationships." When students understand this concept, there should be positive transfer when the mathematics curriculum shifts to algebraic algorithms in higher grade levels.

- From (New) Learning to New Learning: This kind of positive transfer typically occurs when you scaffold learning for students (see Chapter 5 for a review of scaffolding). *Chunking* is another term that is used as a synonym for scaffolding. When the new learning is abstract (or complex or unfamiliar), you teach one chunk at a time beginning with the concrete (or simple or familiar). Your students learn the first chunk; that helps them learn the second chunk, and that helps them learn the third chunk, etc., as you move their learning in stages from the concrete to the abstract (or simple to complex or familiar to unfamiliar). Positive transfer of new learning then can occur at each step of the scaffolding.

- From Learning to Application: This kind of positive transfer occurs when you move from Students Get Some Stuff (top box) to All Students Do Something With the Stuff (right-hand box).

Summary

Attempting to list and explicate every effective teaching strategy would fill volumes. In this chapter, I have attempted to discuss some of the strategies that will be a part of your daily instruction.

Daily Closure

While not essential, there are benefits to bringing each day's instruction to some kind of logical, meaningful ending.

- Check for understanding and inform subsequent instruction.
- Emphasize key information.
- Tie up loose ends.
- Correct misunderstanding.
- Summarize, review, and demonstrate their understanding of major points.
- Consolidate and internalize key information.
- Link lesson ideas to a conceptual framework and/or previously-learned knowledge.
- Transfer ideas to new situations.

Questioning Strategies

Questioning is the tool that may be at the very heart and soul of teaching. Questioning helps you check for understanding, probe thinking, drive the cognitive level of student thinking to higher levels, and keep them engaged and participating. While I have offered a number of principles of questioning for you to consider, there is rarely an *always* or a *never*—that's what principles are.

<u>Feedback</u>

Feedback in this chapter focused on feedback on student learning <u>during</u> instruction. When students are correct, your feedback needs to convey that they are successful and help them understand why they are successful. It also adds to the positive nature of your learning environment. The most difficult aspect of providing feedback is responding to students who are struggling and are not being successful. It is essential that you provide corrective feedback in ways that preserve the students' dignity and sense of self-esteem.

<u>Retention and Transfer of Learning</u>

These two issues clearly are linked. If there is no retention of learning, there can be no positive transfer. The more actively students are participating in the learning, the more likely that they will retain it. When they are enjoying what they are learning and when they see relevancy to what they are learning, the greater the possibility that the brain produces the chemicals that allow dendrites to grow and to connect to other dendrites. When you plan a rigorous, relevant, and enjoyable "right-hand side" of the lesson cycle, your students have multiple opportunities to Do Something With the Stuff and cause the brain to create even more connectivity, organization, and retention.

While T-TESS does not directly address principles of questioning, closure, feedback, retention and transfer, these issues are implied throughout the descriptors.

As you begin to think about these effective teaching practices, ask yourself these questions:

- What can I plan for daily and/or lesson closures?
- Is my goal to check for understanding, emphasize key information, tie up loose ends, correct misunderstanding, summarize/review, consolidate and internalize key information, link lesson ideas to a conceptual framework and/or previously-learned knowledge, and or transfer ideas to new situations?
- What specific strategy/activity will I use?
- What questions can I plan or anticipate to:
  - Maximize the participation or all students?
  - Check for understanding?
  - Stimulate/probe for high level student thinking?
- What feedback strategies can I use to appropriately and positively reinforce student participation and success?
- When students are struggling or unsuccessful, what corrective feedback strategies can I use to support them in ways that advance their learning, preserve their dignity. and preserve their sense of self-esteem?

- What can I do or cause to happen to maximize retention and transfer of their learning?
  - Make the lesson interesting/engaging/fun to maximize their brains' ability to retain learning?
  - Create activities, especially on the right-hand side of the Red Neck Lesson Cycle (Students Doing Something With the Stuff) to promote depth, complexity, and connectivity of learning? Descriptors from Texas

Teacher Evaluation and Support System (T-TESS) Related to Effective Teaching Practices

From the T-TESS Scoring Guide

Dimension 1.1:

- All activities, materials and assessments are relevant to students.
- Provide appropriate time for lesson and lesson closure.

Dimension 1.3: All lessons … connect to students' prior knowledge and experiences.

Dimension 1.4: Questions … encourage all students to engage in complex, higher-order thinking.

Dimension 2.1:

- Addresses student mistakes and follows through to ensure student mastery.
- Provides students opportunities to take initiative of their own learning.

Dimension 2.2:

- Integrates learning objectives with other disciplines.
- Provides opportunities for students to use different types of thinking (e.g., analytical, practical, creative and research-based).

Dimension 2.3:

- Establishes classroom practices that provide opportunities for most students to communicate effectively with the teacher and their peers
- Asks remember, understand and apply level questions that focus on the objective of the lesson and provoke discussion.
- Uses probing questions to clarify and elaborate learning.

Dimension 2.4:

- Adapts lessons to address individual needs of all students.
- Regularly monitors the quality of student participation and performance.

- Provides differentiated instructional methods and content to ensure students have the opportunity to master what is being taught.

- Recognizes when students become confused or disengaged and responds to student learning or social/emotional needs.

Dimension 2.5: Consistently invites input from students in order to monitor and adjust instruction and activities.

Dimension 3.3: Engages all students in relevant, meaningful learning.

Works Referenced

Masterminds, llc (2001). *Corrective feedback*. Retrieved from http://www.calhoun.k12.al.us/makes%20sense/Adobe%20Reader/DO%20NOT%20OPEN%20program%20files/Skill%20instruction/HOW%20to%20teach%20skills/During%20Tactics/SKILL%20Feedback.pdf

Baldwin, T.T. and Ford, J.K., (1988). "Transfer of training: A review and directions for future research." *Personnel Psychology* 41.

Collins Dictionary of Medicine. (2004, 2005). Retrieved December 10 2017 from https://medical-dictionary.thefreedictionary.com/dendrite

Envision, (September 14, 2015). *The science of learning part 2: how the brain learns*. Retrieved from https://www.envisionexperience.com/blog/the-science-of-learning-how-the-brain-learns

Fredrickson, B. L. (2001). "The role of positive emotions in positive psychology: The broaden-and-build theory of positive emotions." *American Psychologist*, 56.

Hestwood, D. and Russell, L. (2007). How your brain learns and remembers. Retrieved from http://www.cabrillo.edu/~grodriguez/Brain_PowerPoint_Gabby.pdf

Hunter, M. (1984). *Reinforcement*. TIP Publications: El Segundo, CA.

Hunter, M. (1987). *Teach for retention*. TIP Publications: El Segundo, CA.

Hunter, M. (1983). *Teach for transfer*. TIP Publications: El Segundo, CA.

Maslow, A. (1943). *A Theory of Human Motivation*. Reprinted 2003 by Watchmaker Publishing, S. E. Ocean Shores, WA.

Simons, P. R. J. (1999). "Transfer of learning: paradoxes for learners." *International Journal of Educational Research*, Vol. 31, No. 7. Retrieved from http://www.learnersdictionary.com/definition/retention

Skinner, B. F. (1972). Beyond freedom and dignity. New York: Vintage Books.

Skinner, B. F. (1948). Walden two. New York: Macmillan and Company.

Spectrum Intervention Group. (December 6, 2011) *Positive vs. corrective feedback*. Retrieved from http://www.spectrumig.com/autism/positive-vs-corrective-feedback/

Epilogue

In 1997, The Texas State Board for Educator Certification (SBEC), created what was then and still is one of the most powerful documents about teaching and learning that I have seen. I offer for your reflection the sections of Curriculum (Knowledge) and Instruction. Note particularly that the language uses the term "Learner-Centered." Learner-centeredness (as opposed to teacher-centeredness) has been the guiding principal that I have attempted to convey in this book.

LEARNER-CENTERED SCHOOLS FOR TEXAS A VISION OF TEXAS EDUCATORS

LEARNER-CENTERED KNOWLEDGE

The teacher possesses and draws on a rich knowledge base of content, pedagogy, and technology to provide relevant and meaningful learning experiences for all students.

The teacher exhibits a strong working knowledge of subject matter and enables students to better understand patterns of thinking specific to a discipline. The teacher stays abreast of current knowledge and practice within the content area, related disciplines, and technology; participates in professional development activities; and collaborates with other professionals. Moreover, the teacher contributes to the knowledge base and understands the pedagogy of the discipline.

As the teacher guides learners to construct knowledge through experiences, they learn about relationships among and within the central themes of various disciplines while also learning how to learn. Recognizing the dynamic nature of knowledge, the teacher selects and organizes topics so students make clear connections between what is taught in the classroom and what they experience outside the classroom. As students probe these relationships, the teacher encourages discussion in which both the teacher's and the students' opinions are valued. To further develop multiple perspectives, the teacher integrates other disciplines, learners' interests, and technological resources so that learners consider the central themes of the subject matter from as many different cultural and intellectual viewpoints as possible.

LEARNER-CENTERED INSTRUCTION

To create a learner-centered community, the teacher collaboratively identifies needs; and plans, implements, and assesses instruction using technology and other resources.

The teacher is a leader of a learner-centered community, in which an atmosphere of trust and openness produces a stimulating exchange of ideas and mutual respect. The teacher is a critical thinker and problem solver who plays a variety of roles when teaching. As a coach, the teacher observes, evaluates, and changes directions and strategies whenever necessary. As a facilitator, the teacher helps students link ideas in the content area to familiar ideas, to prior experiences, and to relevant problems. As a manager, the teacher effectively acquires, allocates, and conserves resources. By encouraging self-directed learning and by modeling respectful behavior, the teacher effectively manages the learning environment so that optimal learning occurs.

Assessment is used to guide the learner community. By using assessment as an integral part of instruction, the teacher responds to the needs of all learners. In addition, the teacher guides learners to develop personally meaningful forms of self-assessment.

The teacher selects materials, technology, activities, and space that are developmentally appropriate and designed to engage interest in learning. As a result, learners work independently and cooperatively in a positive and stimulating learning climate fueled by self-discipline and motivation.

Although the teacher has a vision for the destination of learning, students set individual goals and plan how to reach the destination. As a result, they take responsibility for their own learning, develop a sense of the importance of learning for understanding, and begin to understand themselves as learners. The teacher's plans integrate learning experiences and various forms of assessment that take into consideration the unique characteristics of the learner community. The teacher shares responsibility for the results of this process with all members of the learning community.

Together, learners and teachers take risks in trying out innovative ideas for learning. To facilitate learning, the teacher encourages various types of learners to shape their own learning through active engagement, manipulation, and examination of ideas and materials. Critical thinking, creativity, and problem solving spark further learning. Consequently, there is an appreciation of learning as a life-long process that builds a greater understanding of the world and a feeling of responsibility toward it.

Source: SBEC publication, Learner-Centered Schools for Texas, A Vision of Texas Educators, July 1997